A Voice from Heaven

GERALDINE M. COOL

 www.trafford.com

North America & international
toll-free: 1 888 232 4444 (USA & Canada)
fax: 812 355 4082

CONTENTS

DEDICATION

I WANT TO DEDICATE THIS book to my younger sister, Faith Marie, who withstood many years of hardship and pain. Two weeks after she turned 50 she died from cancer. She had fought cancer 4 times and at last the Lord said it was time to come home. She died February 25th at 4:30 am.

FOREWORD

ALTHOUGH MANY YEARS HAVE passed since her death, I sometimes feel that my sister, Faith Marie, left our family only yesterday.

The memory of Faith has never dimmed, nor has the pain of losing her diminished to any degree. I never want the pain of losing her to vanish.

As the years have gone by I have learned to live with the pain, but honestly I have to confess that there was something seriously lacking in me as a sister.

I have but to close my eyes to picture my joy at having Faith as a sister. She was five years younger than I.

From the very start her life was rough. The day of her birth which was difficult because of a dry birth. When she finally came home and was laid in her crib a special light fell on her face. I observed that she had a pretty face but her features seemed different. She was a very small baby with hardly any hair, had deep blue eyes that could melt the coldest heart.

Deep within my heart I believe God spent her to us to strengthen us spiritually and to draw us closer together in the knowledge, love and fellowship of God.

It has been said that tragedy and sorrow never leave us where they find us. I am grateful to God for the privilege of learning some great lessons of truth through this messenger. She taught us that there is nothing in life that we can not talk to talk to our Heavenly Father about. He knows everything and knows what is in our hearts even before we ask. But he wants us to come to him as a friend and talk with him.

Through the conversation we had she taught me how to live life while on earth in order to achieve higher levels of spirituality as I continues on my heavenward journey. She told me what little time we have left to prevent the worst calamities of prophecy from happening.

CHAPTER 1

The Earliest Messages

*O**H!*** FATHER, IT IS so good to be home. I thought you had forgotten me and my suffering down here on earth. Fifty years up here seems like but a moment but on earth it was a very long, long time and the going was often hard.

When you lifted me up from earth on this early Wednesday morning it was the end after a long courageous battle with cancer. Once you held out your hands, that early morning, I grasped them and went home with you. Now I was free, free from the pain and agony. It was a feeling of relief. No more suffering. What a glorious feeling.

For a split second everything seemed sad and confused but all of a sudden it was bright and clear and I was engulfed with your love. Lord, was it the same for the ones I left behind? Now I'm rid of the hindering clay and am perfectly fine.

The heavenly music is so much nicer than anything I heard on earth. On earth I had as much music as I had pain. I often wondered why I had to suffer so enduring chemotherapy, baldness and nausea. But Lord through it all I felt your presence.

Lord, I am perfectly all right now and rid of the thing called cancer that ate away at my body.

Lord, you came and lifted me up and that was a joyous moment. Everything was bright with light and there was a sound like the rustling of a million angel wings and there was singing everywhere. My old clay shell just fell off and my heart began beating strong and steady and my body was free of pain. Family and friends there are many mansions in heaven.

A ROOM for:

> *The strong*
> *The sick*
> *The healthy*
> *The weak*
> *Those born with ten talents*
> *Those born with one talent*
> *The rich*
> *The poor.*

There is a room for everyone and something to do in that room for you.

Lord, we taught them to see the purpose in pain and the messages on the crosses they have to carry around.

Don't worry, don't cry, God is taking good care of me. Family, pray and trust God. I was with God before I was a sister, daughter, wife or mother to you.

Before her death Faith Marie revealed to us that she had a dream. In this dream she had died and had tried to contact us but no one heard her. This made her very frustrated because there were things that she needed to tell us. Of course, we made fun of the dream because we were determined not to let or allow any negative thoughts to influence us.

As Faith lay dying, with the cancer eating away at her body, the home nurse felt like it wouldn't be long before the family had to say good-bye.

The phone rang at Rebecca's home about 4:30 am on a Wednesday morning informing Becky that Faith was failing fast and was not expected to live more than a few hours. Becky laid in bed thinking about Faith and within a couple hours she got the call that Faith had died. Within Becky's heart there was emptiness and sadness because it was now to late to communicate with Faith. To this day Becky has regretted not communicating with Faith more.

A smell of roses permeated Becky's bedroom the moment she was informed of Faith's death.

The day of the funeral Becky had an out of the body experience and it was like she was there in person. The church was packed with family and friends. When Becky got to the casket she leaned down to say good-bye and as she did she could hear her sister say 'I Love You, sis.'

In the following days Faith revealed to Becky that when she stepped on the streets of gold everyone was busy. Orientation was taking place for souls who were being shown what they had and had not accomplished in their life.

This is a well organized place, very beautiful and peaceful. You cannot imagine how beautiful it is without being here since being here I have learned so much but there is so much more to learn. We remember everything we are taught.

When service is given from the heart it is equivalent to money in heaven. Every time I helped someone I was given a star in my crown. Helping others is the reason I am allowed to study at this retreat.

The earth needs more souls who are willing to serve and fewer who are so willing to judge.

Service transforms the server. Love should be our immediate response to all people, not judgment, not hatred, not envy, *but love.*

Life is meant to be lived for God.

Always ask this questions:
    Is this God's will?
    Would God approve of this?
    Will God be honored by this action?

If the answer to these questions is no than do not do them. We have lost our center, which is God.

Life would be much simpler, much less painful and far more peaceful if we put God first.

Faith! Do you eat in heaven?

Yes, the meals are spectacular and the drinks are like essences of any fruit or vegetable you can imagine. Everything we consume is light, not heavy or dense in any way. There are regular meals and often banquets. The food is different than anything on earth and and so much better. Eating here does not have the importance as it does on earth but it is an important ritual and seems to be enjoyable.

BODY TEMPLE

The body is meant to be treated as a temple. This acquires attention to diet, exercise, spiritual practice, general hygiene and appearance.

How would you show up for work if you worked for God, the master? God should be your first employer.

Diet affects the state of health of you entire body. For you to have a healthy diet takes knowledge of nutrition and attunement to your needs.

Exercise gives energy to your cells and is necessary for the body. It is like a boost. It is not indulgent but necessary for your body to hold maximum light.

When something is holy we treat it with respect and care. We honor it and are grateful to have it in our midst. So it should be with our temples because they house the living spirit. If we neglect to take care of our temples they will deteriorate with a vengeance we should be living longer and stronger than we are.

My body simply gave out and I could no longer fight the battle. I was impatient in many situations and I got myself into stressful situations.

One way to honor the holy temple, of the body, is to address anything that is out of alignment. You cannot shut the door on your psychology and think you are living in harmony with the law.

Spiritual practice is the driving force that helps propel light through the body. It nourishes the cells and provides holiness when the system is ready to be holy. It must be genuine and must be purely motivated. It must be desired, not imposed and should be a constant in a person's life.

Attention to hygiene and appearance is simply respecting the vehicle you were given. 'Cleanliness is next to Godliness.,' is true the right thing to do is to stay clean and make the most of your appearance. But!! Something is out of balance if these things dominate your time or thought

Light gives the person more beauty than anything that could be purchased. Cleanliness keeps earthbound spirits from becoming attached to you and sapping you light and strength.

CHAPTER 2

Experience of Transition

$\mathcal{F}$AITH: WHAT HAPPENED AT the time of your transition?

It may be challenging for some who read this to understand the things I saw. You read of people who have went through tunnels on their way to heaven, but that wasn't the case with me. One minute I was earth bound and the next I was standing at heaven's gates.

Becky I was greeted by an magnificent angel being who welcomed me by my first name and stated that he would be accompanying me on my journey. There are bands of angels who help specially with the transitions of light-bearers.

I ask her if this meant I would not be returning to earth. Simultaneously I would look back at my body and realize it could no longer provide a home for me.

There is a freedom you experience that makes you realize just how form fitting and restricting the body is. We must be grateful for our bodies and treat them with respect.

I regretted that I hadn't put more things in place for the family. She embodied the comfort flame along with the presence of love and gentle wisdom. In her presence I could not doubt anything.

The angel assured me that my family would be able to manage and you would be protected and guided.

Upon my arrival I did not immediately see any family or friends but later I was united with some and told where others were.

Many souls have been re-embodied. It is my understanding that a soul who does not understand re-embodiment is initially permitted to be reunited with some family and friends. Later the soul is tutored in the concept of re-incarnation.

One of the first souls I was allowed to see was Angel Renee who had died within the first two years of her life. She was no longer a mongoloid but a very beautiful girl. Even after all the years that had passed she knew who I was. She ran up to me and said, "Welcome Home, Mother."

The spiritual realm is much more magnificent but also much more complex than I had imagined. There is heaven but heaven has many layers, levels or octaves. People do not all go to the same location.

What you find within the category of heaven are different heavenly levels with heavenly retreats. These retreats are run by angels or ascended hosts.

Within what we have called 'hell' there are multiple levels of the astral plane, including hell itself. Each level going down in vibration intensifies in its severity and in the defiance of the soul sent there. In the heavenly plane each level going up intensifies in light and in the spiritual purity of the souls there.

For each soul the exact amount of blue and pink is mixed with violet. Violet is the wavelength of Gods' light that changes muddy, polluted energy into clear light. Blue is the color of Gods' will and pink is the color of Gods' love. Everyone I seen appeared at their best with more height and a much younger look. Appearance is a product of consciousness in heaven.

I had wasted most of my life with fear, impatience, anger and self-pity which became very vivid as I was allowed to review my life. I am grateful for the times I served with an unselfish heart and for the times I had loved and honored life and I sure was grateful for the honest choices I made.

When I first arrived in heaven the absolute love and care given to me in every way was astounding. I was given baths of light with the violet flame.

The baths were prepared by master alchemists to provide the exact amount of blue or pink color in the violet that each soul needs.

Let me clarify what the violet flame is. It is a unique spiritual energy that can help in all areas of your life. It can heal emotional and physical problems, improve your relationships, help you grow spiritually or to make life easier. The flame is the essence of a unique spiritual light. The spiritual light splits into seven colors, or rays each of which has specific divine qualities. The violet flame comes forth from the violet ray, which has the qualities of mercy, forgiveness, freedom and transmutation. The color violet has been associated with spirituality. It has the highest frequency in the visible spectrum, violet is at the point of transition to the next octave of light.

Ever wish there was a way you could wipe out your past mistakes?

While you can't go back in time, the violet flame has the power to erase, transmute the cause, the effect and even the memory of the past mistakes. Transmutation means to change, to alter in form, appearance or nature. The violet flame changes negative energy into positive energy, darkness into light, "fate" into opportunity. The flame also erases the resultant "bad karma" of our mistakes.

The law of karma is that our past actions, both good and bad, come back to us. Whatever goes around comes around.

Most people must pay their debt to life, or balance their karma, by selflessly reaching out and helping others, by working through misfortunes that come their way or by passing through diseases or other forms of personal suffering. But with the violet flame it doesn't have to be that way because the violet flame is able to transmute or mitigate our negative karma before it comes back to us.

On the physical level, the violet flame can help heal our bodies by removing the karma that makes us vulnerable to illness and disease. But the real cause of disease is often rooted in our mental, emotional and spiritual states.

More and more we are discovering how our emotions and thoughts can affect our health. Hatred and other negative feelings and thoughts actually create excess amounts of acid in the body that cannot absorb. These negative thoughts and feelings often originate in psychological and emotional problems, but the violet flame can help resolve them. When the healing balm of the violet flame is applied the scars of old hurts and painful memories can be healed and dissolved.

How the Violet Flame Works

The violet flame works by changing vibrations. The violet flame works by changing vibrations.

Atoms are mostly empty space and in this space our negative energy and karma gets stuck. When the atoms in our bodies and auras become clogged with this negativity, the electrons whirl slower and slower and we begin to resonate more with negativity and less with light thus we have a lower vibration and become less spiritual.

The negative energy is transmuted by the violet flame. This violet flame does not simply surround and remove the energy but transforms it into light. Because there is less density, within the atom, the electrons whirl faster and faster, raising our vibrations.

There is more spiritual energy in our bodies when we have a higher vibration. The violet flame frees up energy and re-establishes harmony and equilibrium, propelling you into a more spiritual state of being.

How to Use the Violet Flame

The violet flame is easy and practical to us.

The first thing you need to do is call for spiritual protection before invoking the violet flame. Find a place where you will not be disturbed and sit comfortably in a straight back chair with your spine and head erect, legs and arms uncrossed and feet flat on the floor. Rest your hands on your upper legs with palms facing upward.

The violet flame is invoked by repeating a unique form of spoken prayer using meditation and visualization. One of the simplest decrees to the violet flame is: "I AM a being of violet fire! I AM the purity God desires! Take a few, slow deep breaths and center in your heart. Start out slowly giving the decree with love, devotion and feeling. Repeat the decree three or nine times when you first start, then you can gradually increase this to 36, 72 or even 144 repetitions. Repeating this decree strengthens its power and draws more light. You can close your eyes while giving the decree and concentrate on visualizing the violet flame once your are familiar with the decree. Visualize yourself before a huge bonfire and in your imagination color it violet and undulating in endless shades of violet with gradations of purple and pink. So that the violet flame is where you physically are, step into the flame. With these flames curling up from beneath your feet, passing through and around your body, clear over your head, see your body as transparent.

Decreeing is meant to be fun so be creative and use your imagination.

The violet flame appears as a physical violet flame to those who have developed their spiritual sight.

This violet flame can also be used to help family and friends. Visualize the violet flame around them while you are giving the decree and add a prayer before you start. "I thank you and accept it done according to the will of God."

A few minutes of violet flame will produce results, but persistence is needed to penetrate age-old habits you would like to change. In the morning start with a few minutes of violet flame to get you through the day and again in the evening to get you through the night.

The ascended masters teach that violet is the wavelength of God's light that transmutes muddy, polluted energy into clear light. Blue is the color of God's will and pink is the color of God's love. Therefore, the blue side of violet would contain more of the aspects of God's will, the pink side would contain more of God's love.

Everyone appears at his best with more height and a more youthful look than those of us who have just left earth at an advanced age.

In heaven it seems, at least, that appearance is a product of consciousness.

My entire life was shown to me early on and everything was so vivid. Every moment spent in impatience, fear or self-pity seemed so wasted.

Some important question was asked:

How did you use the hours of your life?

How much of your life have you served God in your fellowman and you day to day actions?

How is your capacity to love?

You are shown past lives where you can see most clearly the origin of many of your habit patterns and the reasons for many of the events that took place in your life. There is a recording angel and nothing is missed. We only fool our human self by our actions. In reality, deep inside the soul, it knows what is right or wrong but many try to deaden themselves to it's voice.

During the review of my life I was allowed to know what karma I had needed to balance and what I did balance. The whole tone of the review was loving and positive, not judgmental. It was a time of great learning for my soul. In many ways you are your own judge, for you can see where you have erred.

A helpful exercise for each of you would be to run the film clips of your life, so to speak, and begin to look at how you have been utilizing your life. Notice the progress you have made. Maybe you are a different person than you were ten years ago and that counts for much in heaven.

Do not get struck in self-reproach. Make each day count towards the new direction that you want to take. Extra points are given for lessons you have genuinely learned and tests you have passed, even if not on the first try.

I think of ways to help people keep co-measurement with God. One thing that might help is to remember everything happens for a reason. <u>There are no coincidences</u>. Do not spend your time condemning a difficult person who enters your life but rather ask yourself, is there anyone that I'm allowing to keep me from my spiritual progress because I cannot forgive him. Do not condone the person's actions but stay alert to the possible test of your harmony and balance. My salvation was that I never hold a grudge or spend hours focusing on others treatment of me.

Many life events are shattering to the soul. Some we impose on ourselves and others are imposed on us.

A child who is abused will have this fragmentation occur. That is why, even with therapy, without the understanding and giving of decrees it may take years for such a person to feel whole and they may not feel 100% healed. The therapy is critical but not always sufficient for complete healing to occur.

Soul retrieval (is the energetic essence of your being) can accomplish a level of healing that few other spiritual practices offer. This combined with the use of the violet flame would be most helpful for the individual who has suffered abuse. Most of us can feel this fragmentation when incidents occur. This is a sign to you that soul retrieval is necessary.

As to the burning you felt, you were given an infusion of light during the period of your decrees to help sustain you through what was to come. Such is the love of God for the devout soul.

Twin flames (married couple)

In the beginning two souls were created as one Spirit, but it is possible to be kept from your ascension by the other soul.

Angels work very hard trying to unite souls who are meant to be together in their earthly embodiment or even to interact for a short period of time.

CHAPTER 3

Somemore Early Messages

*I*N HEAVEN THERE ARE no denominations. Denominations are not necessary wrong, but when they become divisive and hateful they lose access to the blessings of God.

A prayer is a devout petition, entreaty or a sending of love and thanks to God. A decree is a command or order given in the name of God and the Christ for the will of God to come into manifestation.

Isaiah 45: 11: "Concerning the works of my hands, command ye me."

Decrees can be powerful tools to call angels into action in the earth.

Praying and Decreeing

These are like fuel in your tank. They prevent many negative things from happening while allowing other positive things to happen. We can 'look down' and immediately tell those who decree from the heart. They have an extra light and protection about them.

It is important to know that many people who consider they are on the spiritual path do not exude this light. They try to hide behind their prayers or decrees and spiritual practices, but they are not honest with themselves or God.

You cannot gossip one minute and decree and pray the next. You cannot hate and yell in anger one minute and call on God the next. All of these habits are indications of an unresolved psychology on the other side.

It is much harder here. We can see everything but we are dependent on situations that will allow us to work things out. When you are in embodiment you have constant opportunities to change, to select the higher path, to address your psychology. And yet many remain blinded to their bad habits as I did.

On this side we must pray for opportunities to serve that will allow us to transcend these momentum. Our progress sometimes comes through others here and then sometimes our progress depends on the opportunity to serve all of you. Therefore we need your prayers. That is why some of us have no choice but to re-embody.

Labor: The master helps us to see the utter importance of striving for excellence in all that we do. If life is meant to glorify God, then the more we strive for excellence the more we are able to be one with the mind of God. We have never lived at a time when fewer people have been aware of this law. We have become a society of expedience, convenience, deception and harried lives.

Failure is not the problem but failing to strive for the highest allows the consciousness to accept lesser and lesser standards for day to day living. With this comes a general decline.

Modern music and drugs have played a major role in this mediocrity. I really believe it has an effect on the angels.

What can be learned here in a day would take a month or more on earth to learn. It is magnificent here but simultaneously I am always aware of the work that needs to be done.

Our loved ones who have gone on before are fully aware of what we say and do.

VIOLET FLAME

The violet flame is an action of the Holy Spirit that changes negative energy into positive. It helps us transmute our negative karma, the record of negative thoughts, feelings and deeds from other lives as well as our own. My mother said in heaven people work with violet flame regularly and said she wished she had been given more violet flame decrees when she was on earth.

A very simple way to invoke the violet flame is to give this mantra a number of times while visualizing spiritual flames of violet hues surrounding your body.

"I am a being of violet flame. I am the purity of God's desires."

This flame has the power to change anything that is negative in our aura it can also transmute national and world karma, mitigate cataclysm and accelerate spiritual development.

Why are people in every nation dealing with so many disasters and illnesses today?

Karma has been descending for centuries but at no other time has the karma returned so swiftly or severely, both for the individual and for the planet. This is creating many devastating situations for people who do not understand the law cycles. New cycles cannot begin until the karma of the previous cycle is completed.

You must prepare for some very hard years on a planetary scale. No one will be totally free from cataclysm and earth changes. What remains to be determined is the nature of war and the possible levels of destruction. A major war can still be averted but the window is closing because fewer people than were expected are responding to the needs of the hour with prayers and decrees.

People's spiritual centers are growing weak instead of strong. Their hearts and minds are focused on the details of daily life on the attainment of human comfortably or in some cases on sheer survival.

The most effective way to transmute karma and avert or mitigate cataclysm and war is the use of the violet flame.

CHAPTER 4

A Master's Retreat

*I*N HEAVEN THERE IS artwork and the beauty is beyond human comprehension. This artwork lifts the spirit. We hear music that accelerates every unit of energy in our beings.

Seeing the here makes me realize how low our standards have fallen in the art that is produced on earth. Much of what is sold and exhibited as art simply out pictures the astral plane and the torment of souls who feel trapped because they are separated from God.

At the highest level, art is meant to reconnect man with God and his true identity. Art is also meant to capture the multifaceted aspects of history and life, pain and suffering as well as joy and overcoming. It was never meant to degrade, distort, or depress the spirit of the person looking at it. Art captures energy. If you feel pain in your third eye, in the center of your forehead, you are not in the presence of anything God inspired. You can tell something about the state of a planet by the art that is being produced. Judge for yourself. What images are we putting before our youth? Do they even know what is possible.?

Many of the walls are made of thin layers of precious gems. Main meeting has thin amethyst walls. The beauty is indescribable and the effect of light on these walls are magnificent. We have a number of rooms and images that are violet in recognition of our mission to share and out picture the violet flames. We also have areas that feature other colors. They are typically iridescent and transcends the hues we are used to on earth.

We have our own rooms and the color of these rooms are determined by our own spiritual needs. If we need to grow on a specific ray it is often out pictured in the color of the room which we are assigned.

The retreat is organized with an efficiency, fluidity and harmony that is almost unknown to us. So much time on earth is taken up satisfying people's egos, desires and little attention is given to the divine plan, the God solution and to the organization. If people could let go and let God be the doer in all aspects of their lives, we would have a golden age.

We are allowed to work on our own pace here and we all report to spiritual directors who help us with our progress.

This retreat contains so much more than we have ever known on earth that it is a bit overwhelming. Souls are very unique both in their attainment and in the momentum they need to overcome.

Until the ascension there are no guarantees of staying on a specific ethereal level unless you continue to transcend yourself. A person arrives at a certain rung of the ladder because he has earned that level but the maintaining or ascending or descending is up to him. The more mastery you earn here the easier it will be to progress if you have to re-embody.

When a person makes their transition, if he is permitted to come to the ethereal level their are four possibilities for his ongoing evolution. These depend on his attainment and the nature of his karma.

A) First possibility is that he will definitely need to re-embody. The prayer in this case is that he may be born to a family of great light and spiritual understanding.

B) Second is that he may have to re-embody but by an extraordinary effort of service and transmutation he may be permitted to stay in the ethereal retreats and become a candidate for the ascension.

C) Third is he does not have to re-embody and is definitely a candidate for the ascension even though the ascension may not take place for some time.

D) The final and most desired possibility is that he makes his ascension and never has to re-embody again.

You must know the light of Jesus never fails. When it is directed into a situation or condition it always has an effect. What is important is the focus or prayer that direct that light. If you could see the light as some can, you would see it being released and adjusted according to the will of God.

Karma is considered and weighed, sometimes on individual scale and sometimes on a national planetary scale. The light may be allowed to lessen or ease a situation but not entirely change it because the life stream must work through the particular karma in order to learn an important lesson. Otherwise the light would be allowed to reverse the condition completely.

People may get into an accident and the perfect individual is at the scene to assist them or even to save them. All of this is the light of God. It never fails to do what the law can allow, even the karmic equation of the particular situation.

The saddest thing is to watch people who feel that God has abandoned them. God never abandons anyone but many abandon God due to their bitterness and hurt. People want God to stay with them through every wrong choice they make but when their karma comes due, they blame God.

We are given the chance to create our own debit and credit sheet. The difficulty is that debts come due. Every right action that we have taken helps us and may give us some mercy but it cannot erase the whole debt.

The lesson is in the light; faith and understanding with which we triumph over our hard times.

Look deep into your soul and ask yourself: Is there anything that I am blaming God for? What will it take for me to let go of this? The more you become one with the light, the more you will understand that it never fails.

CHAPTER 5

Magic Elixir

THE POWER OF THE violet flame. If I had discovered the violet flame and was thinking as an entrepreneur it would be equivalent of finding a marketable fountain of youth.

The violet flame is a multifaceted flame. If it were a product we would be saying; "Get seven for the price of one, Seven unique uses for one purchase price, *Mercy, Forgiveness, Freedom, Opportunity, Alchemy, Diplomacy and Transmutation.*"

I think that if any aspect of the violet flame is neglected, it is the flame of opportunity. Many souls rarely think to invoke the flame of opportunity which can help open the door to new options because they want new or different jobs.

The violet flame is perhaps the greatest dispensation you have been given.

The violet flame at its most powerful is the greatest gift because it can change atoms and electrons.

Jesus used the violet flame in many of his miracles. Purple has been thought to be both a royal and holy color. The gifts of the Holy Spirit are tied to this flame. If you have an illness the violet flame can reverse the entire condition, unless the illness is a karmic necessity for your spiritual evolution. The masters believe in seeking the consultation of a doctor. It may be a person's karma to go through treatment, including surgery and medication. The violet flame can assist in the speed of recovery and the success of any procedure.

Psychological therapy helps people to understand what is behind some of their behaviors, fears, moods or anger. The violet flame then helps to dissolve the cause and core of these behaviors.

We are accountable to wrestle with our emotions and to come into harmony concerning the events and choices of this lifetime. If we do this, God in his infinite mercy will help us change patterns from past lives that we do not remember or understand in our outer consciousness. Any condition that troubles a person whether it be political, financial, medical or psychological will always receive benefit when we send violet flames into its cause and core.

The violet flame is the foundation for the new age. We will enter this age successfully only to the degree that we comprehend and utilize this flame.

The opinion of others, the recognition of others, worldly success and success is worth nothing here. You are measured by your heart and the degree to which you have advanced in compassion, wisdom and the use of God's power.

This does not mean that certain things are wrong. The masters honor beauty and lovely surroundings and you are meant to fulfill you dkarma or divine plan in the earth plan. But it is when the material starts to overtake the spiritual that the soul moves into jeopardy. The fallen angels are masters of subtlety in tempting us with the things of the world. They get you not with the obvious but with the subtlest of compromises and then they expand the wedge inch by inch.

It is not helpful or healthy to live with a sense of burden or unworthiness. The masters rejoice at every step you take in the right direction and they allow for your need to follow certain detours. They weep to see how hard it has become for those on earth to internalize and live the way God wants.

Pray for the violet flame to lift and dissolve all illusion upon the light-bearers and all false sense of reality.

The violet flame is truly the key to penetrating through the mire of what burdens us.

The violet flame is the magic elixir of this age. It can be used to repair damage to the environment and to clean the water supply.

People have been harsh on Mother Earth. The elemental or natural spirits are literally bowed down by neglect and abuse. The elements are begging for more violet flame.

You must not hesitate to use the violet flame in every room that you enter and in every conversation that we have you can give a call such as: "In the name of the Presence of God and my own Christ self, I ask for the violet flame to clear anything between this individual and me that could interfere with my talking with him this day."

You know what a freshly cleaned room feels like or a newly painted room. Well the violet flame can give this feeling to a hotel room, office, home or hospital room.

Arriving at the retreat I received violet flame baths to help release me from any sense of connection to my earthly body and my ties to the earth. It felt like a total acceleration of my being. The violet flame is the cosmic eraser, the cosmic cleanser and the cosmic regenerator.

Violet is the color of the purified soul chakra. It is located between the base chakra and the solar plexus chakra.

The solar plexus is purple and gold flecked with ruby. The purple is the deep action of the violet flame which is needed to heal the psychology and balance the emotions.

The place for the anchoring of your emotional body is your solar plexus. To find perfect harmony you need to change your negative emotions you will be guided by the golden light of illumination. Because it needs more of the blue of protection the solar plexus is purple.

Your soul needs the violet flame to free it and help raise it to the level of the Christ.

Mercy:

Mercy is a excellence of the violet flame. It is the pink ray aspect of this flame. Everyone should aspire for God-excellence. As I watch people I notice that they are continually praying for mercy but are unwilling to grant it to others.

Remember we all make mistakes and mercy is a welcome healing. Mercy changes the giver as well as the receiver. Mercy is not enabling or sympathetic. Mercy is transformative.

God knows our heart and souls, so he only reveals a certain amount of truths at a time. We never know how much we are not shown and we do not know how much is understood by people. People must earn and be ready for the truths they are shown.

There is a spiritual principle that a pupil must be ready before he receives certain teachings for understanding. On the earth I was exposed to the violet flame but its only now that I truly understand it. In my human mind I was not ready for it as it was out of context with what I knew spiritually. To me, violet was a beautiful color but I did not understand the importance of this flame.

A lot of spiritual seekers have seen the violet flame even though they did not fully know what it stands for.

More people will display the gifts of the Holy Spirit if they fulfill their spiritual destinies. Make the ultimate choice- the path of God or the path of mammon.

There is a spiritual equation. One level must be gained before another level is granted. For all who truly seek with their purest hearts the truth will be made available for God does not release truth indiscriminately but yet it is available to all who truly seek with purest hearts.

Forgiveness

There is another aspect of the violet flame and that is the flame of forgiveness. Most people do not realize that forgiveness is critical. The lack of forgiveness closes the doors to spiritual advancement but true forgiveness unlocks the doors to your Christ evolution. We will all account for all we do and say.

We are to forgive and not judge. For when you forgive you are forgiving the soul of the other so you don't hold back your growth or the growth of the other. Pray fervently for a change of heart, if you cannot forgive, because it creates a point of vulnerability in your psychology.

Here is a violet flame of forgiveness decree:

> *I am forgiveness acting here*
> *Casting out all doubt and fear*
> *Setting men free forever*
> *In fill power, I call For forgiveness every hour*
> *To everyone, everywhere*
> *I cast forth forgiving grace.*

Retribution

Retribution is a necessary part of the spiritual path. You should replace anything you have taken from another person. You should look for a way to shower kindness to anyone you have been unkind to. Look for ways to serve, sponsor life and work against that which you once embraced if you have had an abortion. It is critical that you spend time working against the use of drugs if you once promoted drugs to others or acted as a dealer.

Retribution means you understand and come to terms with your wrong choice of the use of God's energy and now want to make atonement for it. You know the best way to do this is to do the opposite of what you have done that you know was wrong.

We must put all our misdeeds into the fire of transmutation and forgiveness.

The negative act of self-justification can block you from atonement and retribution your ultimate goal is to be free of these burdens, which do not come from the Real Life and to be whole before God.

For healing to occur the repayment should be given freely, not forced, in the heart of the person who has committed the sin. Our souls need mercy and forgiveness.

People have compartmentalized God in their lives. A lot of these people treat their religion as if it were a hobby they practice when convenient or like a sport they play on a regular schedule. Others only call upon God in times of extreme crisis.

God is in everything and is the pure energy of life. The end result, when we remove God from our lives and planet, is deterioration. It was meant for God to be the foundation and framework for everything. Many people have lost their reverence for life in one another and the environment.

Seventh Day

The seventh day was consecrated as a day of re-creation in God. This day was meant to remind us of our origin in God, to give us strength and faith to see us though the rest of the week. This day was intended to be a time for the family and spiritual community to be together. We have taken God out of the seventh day. Spirituality has been replaced by materialism and the price we are paying is enormous.

The ascended hosts will ask a major question and that is: "What will it take to wake people up?"

CHAPTER 6

Meeting the Masters

ITHIN THE CHRISTIAN WORLD the dispensation of Jesus and the true purpose of his mission have not been fully understood. God's teachings have been altered so much that people would not recognize the truth, even if it was in front of their face. They would rather defend what the wolves, in sheep's clothing are saying. Jesus desire is for his light-bearers to be given the full truth but that is impossible because of the altering of his teachings.

Jesus is amazed that so many denominations now exist, each interpreting and explaining his teachings in a different way. Jesus is saddened that he has been isolated in the minds of his followers. People accept a picture of heaven that involves mostly the trinity, the Father, the Son and the Holy Ghost (God, Jesus and the Holy Ghost), but this does not seem logical to him. What he longs for us to understand is that it is not he but the Christ which he embodied that is in fact the open door to heaven.

His mission was awe-inspiring---that of showing mankind their true identity in God.

Philippians 2: 5: says "Let this mind be in you, which also was in Christ Jesus."

People read and hear this but yet do not comprehend it. This verse implies we have a greater accountability for our actions. We are meant to become the Christ. This does not mean in any way that we have come in Jesus attainment or with his mission or with his place before God. It does mean that there is a much higher purpose to life than most people understand.

For our actions we have a greater accountability. It presumes a cleansing of our temples physically, mentally, emotionally and spiritually. Though we may sin, our true identity is in God and not as 'the sinner.' People have become totally separated from their spiritual identity because the identity is so much with their human **self.**

Have you Seen Jesus?

Jesus works tirelessly for the interest of our planet. He is touched by true people, but yet he is saddened that these souls were denied the truth. He is most certainly there when two or more are gathered together.

Matthew 18: 20: "For where two or three are gathered in my name, there am I in the midst of them."

God is determined that we have a chance to know the totality of his teachings.

There are so many Christians who live in imitation of Christ. A minority of Christians who speak by the gift of the Holy Spirit any exhibit many of the gifts. These Christians live with a spiritual fervor and joy that is of God.

Some Christians keep changing churches to find the right minister because their souls seek more but they have not found what they are looking for.

A minister is intended to be a spiritual teacher of his or her flock. It is a calling of God. The minister cannot bring the fruits of the teachings to the congregation if he or she are empty vessels or spiritually bankrupted. These ministers cannot be used of God to inspire or transform souls.

So many dear souls go hungry spiritually because of the minister and try to find human kindness in the church community.

This is not Jesus' desire for his flock. He literally weeps at moments as he surveys the church in total. The light that should be present and tangible in the house of God has grown very, very dim.

Sacred Heart

The Sacred heart of Jesus is meant to be the center of Christianity. This sacred heart is the vessel that has within itself the light essence of Christ. During communion we celebrate the blood and body of Christ.

In our bodies the heart is the pump for the blood. The heart is the pump for pure love and light of Christ in spiritual terms. With his heart we are meant to seek oneness. Our hearts are meant to burn with an all-consuming fire.

Take care of your heart for this is what the Bible tells us. If our heart is not pure and centered, we can create hardness of heart or a weakness of heart. Everything we do will, in the long run, affect every part of the body, the heart, diet, exercise, anger, kind words, love or hate, selfishness, giving, stress or harmony. Our heart spiritually or physically reflects our choice of action.

Ask Yourself:
a)   *Today, what have I done to fed my heart?*
b)   *Today, have I cared for the flame of my heart?*

Jesus was the Messiah. God sent Jesus to bring us the message of salvation for our souls. The message of Jesus has been falsified and changed through the ages by many hands. Scholars are coming up with new versions of the Bible.

Many Christians misunderstand Jesus' teachings and think that it is blasphemous to say that each of us can become the Christ. What they do not see is that this takes a spiritual dedication that few seek or even know to seek.

To purify and merge with the light of Christ we must put on Christ-hood every day and this choice has to be made by the soul. This takes discipline, surrender and sacrifice, charity, wisdom and humility. It takes all that Jesus exemplified. Individual Christ-hood is the expression of thanks.

When you expect divine justice does it really make sense that we have only one chance, one lifetime to both accept Christ and make it to heaven or else be condemned? Look at the great injustices people are born into:

> *some to riches*
> *others to poverty*
> *some to love and kindness*
> *while others to abuse and indifference*
> *some to health*
> *others to illness*
> *any so many, many more.*

A righteous soul will always accept Jesus.

John 14: 6: "I am the way, the truth and the life, no man cometh unto the Father but by me."

Jesus is the open door and the way to God.

If Jesus had so chosen he could have been saved by legions of angels.

Matthew 26: 53: "Thinkest thou that I cannot now pray to my Father and he shall presently give me more than twelve legions of angels."

In heaven there are ascended hosts which merge with Jesus and these hosts revere him for the extraordinary mission he took on.

Do some historical research if you find it hard to believe that people might tamper with the teachings of Jesus. The book of Revelation includes the admonishment that anyone tampering with it would be stricken from the Book of Life. There needed to be one teaching that remained pure. The keys to the age we are in are contained in Revelation.

So many churches today want to make humans feel comfortable. But the equation is not one of human comfort and entertainment. The equation has always been of the light.

Jesus wants to save this planet. He has waited for centuries waiting to see if we would ever wake up to his teachings. He has waited since the beginning of time to see if people would wake up to the truth of his teachings.

All this time Jesus has held a balance for us but he is no longer allowed to carry it in the same way.

God is a generous Father. But the time comes when we must either fall in our unwillingness to see and live the truth or rise to reflect all that we have been given. It is now time for us to carry more of our burdens and people are finding this difficult. The answers are in Jesus' teachings.

God will not permit Jesus to carry our burdens, even though Jesus would be willing. It is time for people to wake up spiritually. We must now do the hard work since we have been given all we need.

We will be able to fulfill our destiny when our burdens are light.

Many people that God can only permit salvation through a belief a in Jesus Christ. What they don't allow for is the timing by which a devout, God-obedient soul can be introduce to Christ. Many dear souls of persuasions accept Christ as they make their transition and see that it is the Christ -self that is the doorway to God.

On earth the flame is opposed. You can hear people crying out for peace, but they live outside the boundaries of peace in both their inner and outer lives. The planet would move in the right direction if people has an inner harmony and peace.

What keeps you from peace? Meditate on this, wrestle with it and bend the forces of anti-peace.

Wisdom is not old-fashioned and it is short supply.

People do not recognize illumination ever when it is in front of their face.

God watches as people leave the path because of anger or hurt due to the disciplines and demands.

The more we learn in the educational system the more you find intellect and human intelligence and less wisdom.

We have lost sight of the true wisdom of leadership which has resulted in not electing wise leaders. People are inclined to think that it is a dream, a false hope, a fairy tale to want a leader who is a good model, who has sincerity, knowledge, honor and compassion. We are losing sight of what is right and possible. We have become cynical.

Of our four lower bodies, the emotional body is usually the hardest for most people.

Our control over our emotions is gained when your attachment to God and to becoming the Christ is greater than any of your desires for the world. Only a few people have this level of commitment to the path. Peoples attachment to the world are still taking precedence over their union with Christ even though they love the path and want to grow spiritually.

When will you declare spiritual warfare on the momentums you are holding back? On what day will you achieve the humility to seek help that you may need, whether spiritually or psychological counseling, or increased work at the altar? To each of these questions the answer is different, but the test is not to deceive yourself concerning your own needs.

For planet earth we must demand a new day. For every problem we face we must call out in prayer for Gods solutions. The angels are awaiting assignments. We need God government on this planet.

There are times when we unknowingly and sometimes consciously, we deny, hide, resent and lie in order to avoid looking at our psychology. These follow us through our lifetimes until one day we stop and say: "My desire is for the peace of Jesus to be within me, his harmony and love. I am ready to face all that has kept me from my real self."

We are inclined to focus on our human relationships but what is the nature of your relationship to God?

What do you blame God for?

What are you angry at God for?

Why do you distance yourself from God?

When do you let God in your life and when do you omit God?

How do you see and understand the Father?

This is the key to your healing.

As you select your activities ask yourself;

Is this how Jesus would spend his time?

It is hard for God to watch the ways people are blinded by their own karma and their false sense of reality. So many people pursue activities that will count for neither good or bad in the heavenly realm.

Many of the teachings are quite simple and yet demand that we fully challenge all that is unreal within ourselves.

The prayer of Saint Francis contains much of what you need to aspire.

Pray to be shown what blocks you from seeing and understanding the greatest amount of the masters' teachings.

Most of us know the prayer of Saint Francis of Assisi. This prayer can be interpreted on two levels. On the first level, if you become or embody all that is in this prayer, you will be like an remedy for evil to all that oppresses eternal life. To all you meet your presence will be similar to a bolt of healing light. With this healing light others will experience love, peace, pardon, faith, light, hope and joy in their interactions with you. Seeing the light in you others will want to know the source of this light and you will be able to instruct their souls.

The second level of this prayer is a personal one in which you study each line looking honestly at where you stand on the characteristics mentioned. Examine what in you finds it hard to exemplify what is being stated.

Lord, make me an instrument of thy peace.

We must radiate and embody all that is included in this prayer to have true peace. You must face all that blocks harmony within you if you are to be an instrument of peace.

Where there is hatred, let me sow love.

You must examine all that is anti-love that is within you, if you are to be an instrument of love.

Where there is injury, pardon.

When we are hurt we must seek pardon, for through pardoning you can sustain love and keep harmony.

Where there is doubt, faith.

Seek to face the core of your doubts, when you have doubt. If you truly embrace it, faith is greater than doubt.

Ask yourself this questions:

Why do I give such power to this particular doubt?

Why do I allow it to be greater than my faith?

Where there is despair, hope.

Remember hope when you are in a state of despair. Despair exceeds the true self. Hope allows you to proceed.

Where there is darkness, light.

Attempt to remember the light in your darkest moments. Light is the alchemical key.

And where is sadness, joy.

Bind all anti-joy energies in your aura or that are being sent against you, when you are sad.

O Divine Master, grant that I may not so much seek to be consoled as to console, to be understood, as to understand.

When we are burdened there is a very good remedy. That is to console another person and try to understand the burdens or pain he or she is experiencing. Don't ignore your own pain for it is critical to face it. Dwelling in your pain day after day increases your burden. To be a service to others is truly a privilege. Please, do not ignore this sacred calling.

To be loved as to love.

More love comes to you when your love is considerate of others. (unselfishly). This is the spiritual law.

For it is in giving that we receive.

You will receive when you give unselfishly. This is a spiritual law.

I*t is in pardoning that we are pardoned.*

More mercy will come to you when you pardon and show mercy to others. It is a spiritual law.

And it is in dying we are born to eternal life.

And in dying--dying to all that is unreal and living the words of this prayer which are real--you are born to eternal life.

CHAPTER 7

Lessons of Lifetimes-- Karma an Reincarnation

*H*AVE YOU NOTICED HOW often the masters have advised you to balance your self-created destiny (karma) while you are in embodiment rather than waiting until you are on the other side. While you are in human form there are literally nonstop opportunities to transmute karma. You are constantly placed in situations with people you need to be with.

When you are not holding on to a particular situation or person due to a lack of harmony or resolution, you are far more free.

While you are on earth you can work out many things, but not all. Some of the works require re-embodiment. Others require enormous service and decree work. In heaven more is ask of you than on earth. While in embodiment your vision is dim and

51

unclear but once you get to heaven you will see clearly what you need to do.

People on earth are angry or resentful of their circumstances. These people never stop to realize that their very salvation lies in overcoming with love that which has been set before him.

In this period of time major karma has come due and people find this hard to understand. Following them for lifetimes people have negative momentums.

<u>Nothing happens without a reason.</u> The divine system is elegant. There is no injustice in heaven--to repeat it---there is no injustice in heaven. If people only knew how many times the angels have tried to intervene on their behalf, how many times their suffering could have been worse, they would kneel in front of God in gratitude.

Pray to be shown your points of vulnerability and be willing to work on them through psychological work and decrees.

There is an important lesson of this lifetime and it is that it matters what company we keep and in what matter we keep the company. When we appoint people to positions of responsibility or select them as our closest friends, we must pray for the discernment of God. The higher we rise in positions of leadership the more responsibility we have for people we surround ourselves with, from whom we take advice and to whom we grant decision making power. No one who truly loves our souls will encourage us to do things that move forward our lower natures and suppress the Christ.

Corruption can be very clever and can wear many facades. Seemingly corruption can cloak itself in friendly, charming and articulate pretenses. It is thoroughly skilled at stroking the egos of others. Pray for the evil ones to be exposed that they may stand naked beside their evil deeds. Pray that you will never be misled or made vulnerable by the needs of the ego.

Many simple people throughout the ages have done more for God than their counterparts who appeared more learned and more prominent before men.

Beware of the subtleties of idolatry and do not miss what you have learned from the messenger. The teachers are way-showers. You must earn your attainment because it cannot be handed to you. The teachers are the models and are examples of what is possible and they offer spiritual tools to help you progress.

CHAPTER 8

Dharma

*D*HARMA IS REFERRING BOTH to the vast law and to the duty of conforming to that law or to your own nature as a showing or manifestation of that law. This term is used to describe the life plan each person is born with.

Many of us do not give priority to seeking their given dharma. You have to fulfill your dharma. You and you alone can contribute in this lifetime. By fulfilling and finding your true dharma, you are helping others because, in a spiritual sense, the plant benefits when individuals connect to that one chord that is theirs to play in this lifetime.

People choose one poorly constructed money adventure after another. A lot of these people mistakenly feel that they have found the perfect way to gain abundance even though the way may be risky, confused and not anchored in wise economic principles. They are hoping to have a quick source of money to help themselves, their favorite cause, their church or others. Theses hopes are lawful but are not anchored in God-reality and the pursuit of dharma is nowhere in the picture.

There will always be those who make investments that lead to great financial freedom and there are others, who by chance, win contests and lotteries. A good majority of us do not fall into these categories. Importantly, investments should not take precedence over own spiritual liberation and dharma.

There are many ways people avoid their dharma. A lot of people simply take the first job that comes to them without effort. While there are others that accept a secure but unfulfilling job and continue in it for years. They are secure but miserable. The spiritual path does demand practicality. People must eat, have clothes to wear and a roof over their heads. Bills must be paid. If you are staying in a non-fulfilling job it could be the call of the hour. Even though you are in a less than fulfilling job keep praying that you will discover your true calling. These things are the Father's great pleasure but we must ask him. Never lose sight of or belief in your dharma.

It is Gods' will that we all find prosperity but spiritual prosperity is the treasure trove from which all else can and will unfold. Pray for good judgment in your work life. Examine the direction in which these motives are taking you and your motives for work. Are you fulfilling your dharma? In fulfilling it there is peace but there is a struggle when it has not been recognized or made known. In recognizing and pursuing your dharma pray for Gods' guidance and direction.

Dharma is not always glamorous nor does it place you in center stage. Serving others in patience, wisdom and loving kindness could be your strong dharma. The the lawful needs of the planet are far-reaching and changing and these needs are our dharma. God does not judge us on fortune or fame but rather on whether we listen to our promptings and place the laws of God first.

Jesus fulfilled the hardest hour of his path on earth when he submitted to the crucifixion. Out of his sacrifice and obedience to Gods' plan, Christianity was given birth.

To fulfill the divine plan of our life-streams we must reflect on our own willingness. When the going is comfortable and does not ask much of us, it is easy to be a follower of the true path. But are we willing to endure the hard times? In order to remain true to our divine plan are we willing to sacrifice the things that mean the most to us?

Every moment of our life we have deciding moments. Only you and you alone know how you have reacted or answered when God knocked. Many people want to know what their dharma is but a good share of them are not willing to do what it will take to fulfill their dharma.

Karma, physical action-self created destiny. No one can escape their karma. We can change it and we may receive dispensations, but one way or another we must deal with it delaying the inevitable only lengthens our own path and provides more opportunities to accrue further karma.

Life is not above making mistakes. Life is about having a willingness to face and right the errors we have made.

People have free will so we are never 'stuck' anywhere by the dictates of God. It is Gods' desire for us to take action by faith. Many of us wait for God to do everything but the test of faith is to acknowledge our prompting from God and take action on behalf of what God is showing us.

After a certain point on our path God does not spoon-feed us. We are advised to put on the mantle of son or daughter of God. Our mantle bears a price and is earned by responding to the inner prompting of the Lord. We cannot ask for divine guidance and then never listen for the answer or act on it.

Change is very difficult for some people. Do not put false boundaries on yourself and do not limit God.

The key is not to be impulsive or change just for changes sake but to talk to God intimately with God and to listen when you have clear promptings. Faith demands hard decisions and at times makes us humans uncomfortable. Faith equates with fearlessness.

Yes, yes and a million times yes, God is practical. Taking a risk may be one way for one soul, the secure job may be the right choice for another. Our answer is always in the heart of our soul when we are willing to pray, fast and seek the counsel of God.

For the most part we create our own prisons and limitations. We are blinded by what we know and blinded in regards to what we are willing to see. Many of us are too impulsive while others are too fearful. On some level we know where we are positioned and what our habit patterns reveal.

Do not be deceived when it appears God is not responding because it might be you who is not responding to his clear answer and signs.

Spiritual Post:

Living we maintain our spiritual post. Putting out a certain wattage and offering light to a specific amount of space, this post is like a lamp. God counts on this guaranteed lamp to help promote his works and to hold the balance of the planet. A persons first calling should be to this post, no matter what an individual is pursuing in terms of career or study. Your light should offer an ever-increasing wattage as you transcend yourself spiritually. Never let it go below the promised amount.

We have many challenges. The first challenge is that we must understand and believe we hold a spiritual post. We must have the ability and discrimination what change means and what it does not mean. In the ways of the world they need to be wise. There are many people losing their spiritual anchoring and yielding to the subtle ways in which the world dissipates light.

Pray that you will be shown your spiritual post and what God counts on you to do everyday. Look within yourself for what you are truly seeking or perhaps what you are running from. If this concept does not appeal to you remember this in Luke 12:48: "From those who are given much, much is required." So that the work of God can manifest on this planet, light is meant to be honored and shared.

When a light burns out in a room that room grows dim and most often, dark. So it is with our planet and the post that you hold.

May your light shine brightly and kindly.

CHAPTER 9

Dealing with Personal Psychology

*I*N RELATION TO THE years we have been on our path it is not unusual for the messenger to tell us that our hearts have not grown. Even if we do all of the right things spiritually we need to face the blocks in our psychology because we often remain stuck at a certain level of the increase of our heart.

Concerning the work of our psychology there are more men than women that choose to ignore the promptings of the master. Do not fear this because it is a step to freedom. In our emotional bodies we all have holes that need repaired. Our psychology needs to be cared for.

There are many clues to unresolved psychology:
a) *constantly critical of others*
b) *specific fears that will not go away*
c) *regularly moody*
d) *subject to anger*
e) *having had a dysfunctional or challenging upbringing.*

These signs and other symptoms will tell us there are pockets of non-resolution in our psychology. To move on with our path we need to resolve these signs and symptoms to have freedom. Your decrees can hasten the whole process and you will likely experience a new level of fire in your heart. The masters do not waste words nor do they sit and chat. There is meaning behind anything and everything they say and there is a message for everyone in their words.

We all have free will to decide what we do and do not need. Pray that nothing will blind you to anything that will help you advance.

The timetables of heaven are different than the timetables on earth. Sometimes what appears to the human consciousness to be a tragedy, is in the divine sense the fulfilling of our self-created destiny. We should not do things for approval or for personal attention but because it is right and worthy before God. No one person is more important than another.

For the people who have power and personal recognition they have the opportunity to exalt the ways of God or to ignore or even slander them. What they do can impact millions.

Matthew 19: 24 tells us "...it is easier for a camel to go through the eye of a needle, than for the rich man to enter into the kingdom of God."

The average person does not realize how unyielding the media can be and how with its power has become great. Often intrigue and corruption are highlighted over good and we receive bias over truth.

There are times where we do not use discernment and where we do not understand our highest truths. No one escapes the all-seeing eyes of God.

For more than one lifetime, unworthiness that will not go away has usually been present. Do not hold on to the unworthiness because it is as if you are saying; 'I believe my carnal mind more than my Holy Christ self.' holding onto unworthiness is a denial of divine justice. Trust that you will be given a chance to work out any violation of Gods' laws. Imposing a life sentence on yourself is not necessary. Ask yourself; 'Why am I unwilling to forgive myself and trust in divine justice?'

There are many ways that we are worthy in the eyes of God.

Try repeating this statement for several weeks and see what happens; 'Christ in me is worthy.' From within and without ask God to remove all sense of unworthiness from you.

There is no way that you can know the many ways that you are worthy before God.

Call for the transmutation of all sense of unworthiness and remember to use the violet flame. Make this call daily. Ask to be shown anything in your psychology that is blocking your freedom from this momentum.

Do not judge yourself or others, this alone is Gods' alone to do. From wherever you are today go forward and do not stay in the past. If you find that you cannot free yourself seek spiritual counseling or guidance. Do not accept unworthiness for doing so you are buying the word of Satan over the word of God.

We are parents of our own soul. Do not believe that; 'Nothing I do, no matter how many decrees, right actions or acts of kindness I perform will not make me worthy.' A sense of unworthiness can lead to a false idolatry of others because you are unwilling to acknowledge your own worth. Dear souls, do not carry this poison of unworthiness.

Many people carry a sense of unworthiness for something that wasn't even their fault. Here are some situations where guilt and unworthiness may arise:

   a)   *a child being abused*
   b)   *if a parent dies when a child is young*
   c)   *if parents argue about children*
   d)   *divorce*
   e)   *if one child is injured and another is spared injury*

There may have been karma that allowed these things to happen to the person but the end result does not mean the recipient was unworthy.

Stand in a room with amethyst walls with saints and hand them your burdens, your bundle of unworthiness and watch the saints cast them into the violet flame once and for all. Now go forward free to serve in the light.

Marriage:

Marriage is a sacrament. It is not to be taken lightly. It is Gods' intention that when people marry they should work out their karma with their mate.

Hebrews 13:4: "Marriage should be honored by everyone, and husband and wife should keep their marriage pure..."

In our current times marriage is taken too lightly. Imagination beyond what is healthy has entered into marriage. A lot of people have lost their commitment to excellence and have lost their understanding of the commitment to bear one another's burdens.

Galatians 6: 2: "Bear ye one another's burdens and so fulfill the law of Christ."

Holding the sinless concept for your partner or thinking of him or her as the Christ is not just a nice thing to do, it is necessary. If we treat our spouses differently we trap one another in their momentums, often complaining and holding a sense of each others faults rather than their God potential.

There are many marriages ending in divorce. Pray hard and long before ending a marriage. Never let involvement with another be the cause of the end of the marriage.

A must in marriage is the ruby-ray, the full power of Gods love, around your relationships daily.

Fewer marriages would end if people were willing to face their psychology. An integrated psychology and spiritual freedom are synonymous. We should guard what we have and decree protection in our marriage. Guard well what God has given you and you will have nothing to fear.

Each marriage is unique before God. God is the only one who can let us know the timing in our lives.

Nothing should be done with haste or without the awareness of the will of God. Finding your true self and resolving your psychology is the greatest gift you can give to your twin flame.

If we are not alert cataclysm will hit us. The fallen ones love to ride the waves of our karma and our vulnerabilities.

Neglect:

To the general duties of life we have a general lack of commitment. Each contract we enter into there must be a sacredness and respect for the relationship.

In today's world people are to caught up in what is not important, forgetting their place of duty while neglecting to honor ones words and obligations.

There must be a sacredness and respect for each relationship we enter.

Neglect breeds mediocrity and finally a lowering consciousness, a reducing of general respect for life and one another. Neglect leads to deterioration.

Most people are not aware that neglect is a crime.

Never promise anything you cannot fulfill but fulfill all your promises.

Constancy (Faithful-Loyal)

Many people ebb and flow. One week they are dedicated to mediating, studying, prayer and facing their psychology but the next week they bow to the demands of daily life, letting their commitments slip.

The masters look for constancy. It is better for us to promise less and be consistent than to promise the world at a moment of spiritual exuberance. Do not fail to fulfill what you have promised.

Each day that we wake up, to the dawn of a new day, it is a new beginning. Do not get locked into feelings of guilt about your past. Atone and move forward. If you live a life of ebb and flow you are vulnerable whereas constancy brings commitment; positive habits are strengthened and growth is possible.

Examine your days. How faithful are you in your service to God and in your spiritual practice? As we travel our journey look for ways to grow that are God-reality. Doing more than you planned is never a problem. If you constantly fail to fulfill what you have promised it makes the masters wonder what you can be trusted with. It is a matter of your word, in the end.

We all have cycles that demand more or less of us. No matter what happens set a minimum commitment that you will not go below and you will find this commitment will help you through the hardest of cycles.

I Am Presence

We are being held back by the lack of true understanding of the I Am Presence, the Spirit-spark and the God within. God has given you a portion of His being that is your true identity and all that God asks of you, in return, is that you desire it above all else and reclaim your oneness with it. If you would go into Gods presence saying, "Go before me into this room and speak through me, I have entered a situation of danger. Take over! I shall not be moved."

Psalms 16; 8: "..I shall not be moved."

These little motivations will change your whole life.

Maintaining Attunement

To be fully present at every moment means to be alert and awake. You will act and answer in a manner that is in full accordance with the will of God. You will be fully present every moment.

When a person gets an unexpected phone call or meets someone unexpectedly they are taken off guard. Being taken off guard they don't always speak or react on the highest level. People are more likely to say what exemplifies Christ when their consciousness is on guard and they are in frequent communion with God. Our goal must be to honor Christ in all interactions and not to protect the human. If we would use this as our motto we would take less but with much more wisdom, love and power when we speak.

Think over your converstions in the last few days and ask yourself:

a) what have you done to honor Christ?
b) What was my state of consciousness?
c) Who was I concerned about?
d) To what degree did I honor Christ?

Chakra:

Any of the seven major energy centres in the body.
They are:

a) *Root chakra at the base of the spine*

b) *Sacral chakra is lower abdomen*

c) *Personal power chakra is above the belly button*

d) *Heart chakra is at the center of the chest*

e) *Throat chakra is true voice*

f) *Intuitive chakra is the inner compass*

g) *Crown is at the tip of the head (chakra of the mind).*

Chakra is rampant because of misuse of the mouth. Think of your words as pearls and treat each word as it were a pearl. Watch very carefully your gossiping, idle talking and swearing. These are misuses of the word and can make you open to attack. Our words are meant to be like cups of light. The words we say are to be used to uplift, praise, educate, enlighten, challenge evil and for many other purposes.

Tied to swear words are entities. If you let the entities grow the happier it becomes, as it can create a home in a persons aura. If you swear in anger it can destroy an entire force field and can put tears in our aura. Swearing from habit will gradually wear away the power of the persons words and aura. When a person swears he is keeping company of an entity that wishes to ennoble but would rather destroy. Swearing is like taking willingly on something to destroy you no matter how good you are in other ways.

In anger there is no true power but there is power in harmony and centeredness. Therein lies the strength of the experts.

God rewards those who endure and keep his name while they are persecuted.

Part of the spiritual path is persecution. It comes with many levels of intensity and in many forms.

Matthew 5: 10: "Blessed are they which are persecuted for righteousness' sake; for theirs is the kingdom of God."

For great is our reward.

Many of us feel that a portion of life has been wasted. But this may be the most important accomplishment of our lifetime in spiritual terms.

Mistakes, Sin and Error

When we make a mistake that we consider difficult we punish ourselves over and over internally. In doing this we determine that God is not capable of forgiving us because we never forgive ourselves. Long before we forgive ourselves, the irony is that those things for which we are genuinely repentant are forgiven. This has nothing to do with the karmic payment that may be asked of us in this life or another.

What people rarely contemplate and are far more grievous spiritually are patterns and momentums such as swearing, gossip, anger, irritability and selfishness for which many are never repentant. These momentums hurl energy at others limiting people and their personal spiritual growth far more than one act for which the soul sincerely atones.

We need to pray to be shown the momentums that are holding us back. Some of these can be lifetime old.

Parents are accountable to avoid either overindulging their children or neglecting them. Parents must pray to be wise tutors of their children souls. Each child needs different handling and each child has a unique psychology and their years represent an opportunity to get a helpful beginning on overcoming those momentums that will try to rule his or her present life if they go unchecked or unchallenged. Of every soul with whom you are entrusted it takes a very deep love and patience to work the uniqueness. When this is done it is like gold in your heavenly bank account. A child has free will but the clearness of the messages and parental modeling and discipline received during the child's first twelve years can assist the child through the rest of his or hers life.

Do not hide from your momentums. Seek to identity them and be freed from them loving self-justification, personal and spiritual blindness is the dweller (ourselves). The higher self loves to face anything that will free the soul from the dweller.

The question is; "Which one is running your life?"

As human beings we find it easy to fall into the trap of keeping our own person's dweller peaceful than seeking to reach his higher self. Contemplate your own relationships.

Stop and assess yourself, if you find yourself judging everyone. Stop and look at your own intent if you find yourself suspicious of everyone's intent. Something is wrong if you live a life in which you have no time to help others and everything centers around you.

Fear can:

a) *keep you from living*
b) *blind you to the good in people*
c) *destroy your health and paralyze your feelings*
d) *usurp your dharma and become your master.*

Seeking control and controlling others over the material realm will never put an end to the fear. Fear is dissolved by love and control is dissolved by humility and the love of the higher self. Here is something you need to remember: You are not truly free if you are being controlled or if you desire to control others. If you abide in fear you cannot know true love.

> *Seek God control*
> *God love*
> *and God mastery.*

Anger

Anger must be cleared from a person's being if he or she wants healing, spiritual victory and personal freedom. Anger is like a parasite that lives off of and depletes a person's light source. Anger can be worn on the surface or buried deep within a person's mind and can make them vulnerable.

No matter which way the person is open to attack the anger which starts before his lifetime are the most difficult cases. Frequently some individuals have carried a core anger for centuries and their anger is with God. Many individuals blame God for their circumstances of their lives. Many of us have failed to defend our faith at a crucial point of time and instead of blaming ourselves we blame God.

Lurking behind anger is fear and hatred. Fear and hatred are flourishing. You would be surprised how much of this could be avoided if people understood the principles of personal responsibility of genuine faith. If people understand this they could cultivate loving kindness in their hearts.

We can rid ourselves of this insidious energy if we pray to be shown any anger in our soul or mind. Ask to be shown the best method to use to rid yourself of this anger. Ridding yourselves of anger will be a combination of spiritual work, therapy and a genuine desire to be healed. Never, never ignore anger. It must be dealt with or anger will deal with you and others who are important to you.

Here are a couple scriptures on anger:

Psalms 37: 8: "Cease from anger..."

Proverbs 16: 32: "He that is slow to anger is better than the mighty..."

Attending services or uttering prayers does not matter if these moments of devotion are lost through angry outbursts, then you are not advancing spiritually. Do not lose what you have gained through anger. Anger does not want to be touched because it likes to control people. It is imperative to break through this force or barrier and begin to unravel its source within us. You are still the angry one even if you believe that others are at fault for creating your anger and must be cleared of this energy. You need to examine the reason why you wish to keep company with this energy, if you are holding onto anger.

What is it hiding?
What is it feeding?

Any power that anger appears to have is empty and misleading. Anger is used to manipulate situations and people, but in the end it has manipulated you into creating more karma.

Anger:
a) *can block the growth of your heart and its ability to love*
b) *can attack your physical heart*
c) *anger is a serious pitfall.*

If you want to free yourself from bondage it is imperative that you face any vestiges of anger that remains within you.

Mastering the Mind

For the sons and daughters of God, why are the temptations of the illusory world so powerful?

Our thoughts have an incredible range, from desires to fear, from criticism to anger and hatred. Also our thoughts can be inventive, creative and hopeful, holy and pure.

True prayer has many levels as does meditation. Get into a meditative position and clear your mind.

Do not give any power to the thoughts that pass through your mind. Meditation teaches you the level of distraction of your mind. To understand your thoughts, watch them, record them for awhile and notice the nature of you thoughts. After this try to achieve a level where your thoughts pass your mind as if they were on a movie screen while you act as observer.

In life we are tossed about by what we allow to control us when in reality the Holy Spirit, not the synthetic self should be in control. Evil is defeated when you do not give it any power. Select a holy affirmative to keep your mind focused on God.

Resist idle conversation. Do not be discouraged from the conversation of family sharing or holy friendship. Family sharing and holy friendship are lawful and should be exalted. As we fulfill some of the necessary tasks of life, do not eliminate the courtesies or the encounters we have with people. The spiritual development of a soul involves thoughts, words and deeds. You are the steward of your own being. Only you in holy honesty know how to handle the thoughts, words and deeds in your life.

Seek to stay in the flame of abundant consciousness free from destructive thoughts. *Stay Anchored!!!!* Much of what you seek and dream of will be yours if you seek this victory.

Spiritual attainment is about changing the four lower bodies. This suggests indirectly that all bad habits and momentums can be overcome. Spiritual attainment is a path and not an instant formula. The timing of God is always based on an equation. In an instant, a miracle may seem to happen, but leading up to that moment is whole spiritual equation. This equation is composed of attainment, mercy, grace and karma.

Anxiety:

Anxiety(troubles or worries) can feel like an internal cataclysm. It is capable of paralyzing people and it can take precedence over all other occurrences in a person's life. For which there is no apparent origin because anxiety seems overpowering and usually has its roots in a in a physical or psychic trauma of a previous life. Other anxieties (troubles or worries) have their roots in a crisis or trauma in this life but people are sometimes not aware that the origin relates to a particular event. Other people have a chemical psychological condition that causes anxiety. Because people want the approval of others for their actions and appearance many anxieties are produced. Our anxiety is representative of our selfishness coupled with a lack of faith in Gods ability to provide for our smallest needs or concerns. Becoming more important than our relationship with God is our human success. As our anxieties increase they become like a volcano growing in intensity as more fear gets added.

For our sanity we must seek the resolution of our minds.

There is something complex to each of us that cannot be handled by two-bit advice. For everyone and anyone there is a divine resolution for us if we earnestly seek wholeness.

Anxiety is typically a focus on the not-self, coupled with a lack of faith in God's ability to provide for our smallest need or concern.

There is a complexity to each person that cannot be handled with two-bit advice. There is a divine resolution for each person who earnestly seeks wholeness.

It is important to be humble enough to seek help when necessary and to conquer these momentums. We should never allow anxiety to become the ruler of our days or the denier of our sleep.

It is my prayer that you may find peace, for it is within each of us.

On the Use of Time

Here are some questions to ask yourself to assess where our energy and time has gone:

a)   *How much time did you spend gossiping?*

b)   *How much time do you spend on the computer?*

c)   *How much time do you spend texting?*

d)   *How much time do you spend being angry or hurt?*

e)   *How much time do you spend learning?*

f)   *How much time do you spend on reading the Bible?*

g)   *How much time do you spend in prayer?*

h) *How much time do you spend watching TV?*

i)   *How much time did you spend in idle conversation?*

j)   *How much time did you spend in helping others?*

k)   *How much time did you spend without meaning or purpose?*

l)   *How much time do you spend on your job?*

If you are honest with yourself patterns will emerge and an improved use of time will be established.

Remember this; if you are side-tracked you are less likely to see and fight the forces of evil that are working overtime to destroy all that is pure, holy and of god. The forces of evil must be dealt with and the planet must be cleared of all the anti-life and anti-light.

Gratitude

Most of us know that it is right to thank others and that it feels good to be appreciated for something you have done or for who you are.

The sheer power of gratitude is most often overlooked or misunderstood.

An open door to God is thankfulness. For everything that is put in our pathway, the good or the bad, we should with grateful hearts thank God. We should be thankful because it is an opportunity to benefit and edify God and to grow spiritually.

Reciprocity is not adequate!!!

Ask yourself this questions:

a) *If I lived in a state of continuous gratitude, what would I be like?*

b) *In my life what am I unable to be grateful for?*

If you sincerely are able to thank God even when difficult things happen to you, it gives you an opportunity to grow. When you struggle or experience pain, you are more likely to move through or out of a situation more quickly than if you are bitter or are questioning Gods' motives or if you are in a state of pity.

When we are spiritually blinded it keeps us from gratitude. The more a person embraces the way of gratitude the more he/she can understand the principles of karma and the divine justice system.

Ingratitude can lead to a bitterness that prevents a soul with substantial attainment from moving forward on the path. If a person dies in the state of ingratitude the soul will be pulled down with this cancer that has been allowed to infest the body and spirit.

CHAPTER 10

Choose Life not Death

HE TAKING OF LIFE through abortion is perhaps the most thankless, ungrateful act and one that has resulted in tremendous weight upon the people here in the United States and many other parts of the world. Untold numbers of lovely and dear souls have been deceived into believing that abortion is a 'right' or 'lawful' choice. God has given us free will, **BUT** does it seem likely it would ever be the will of God for us to take a life?

Each and every one of us are accountable for our decisions. If you make a decision to have sex, you should know the consequences, like diseases and pregnancy. Life is to be loved and respected deeply at all levels.

There are some people that honor the environment and the destruction of earth horrifies them. They fight for many species who are in danger of extinction but they blind themselves to the fact that abortion is also destruction of life. Life is holy and meant to be protected.

Possibly the most forceful understanding comes when you are in the heavenly kingdom and there are souls you meet who are denied embodiment due to abortion, not once, but several times. These souls need the opportunity to advance which requires that they re-embody. The soul selects his/her family, no matter how difficult the soul is prepared to handle the situation. We need to understand the reverence for life. If we contact the true heart of a genuine spiritual path we should know life is holy and must be honored.

There is no denying that life begins at conception but so many feel they have the freedom of choice whether or not life should proceed. Do you know that most abortions are not done until after he first sign of heartbeat is detected? Is this the real meaning of freedom--the killing of a living soul?

If this practice was changed there would be a great burden lifted from the planet.

Here are some reasons that people use to have abortions:

a) *Not ready for the responsibility of parenthood*
b) *Having a child would negatively alter their lives*
c) *Having reputations tinted*
d) *Reaction to their families*

e) *Too many children already*
f) *Not wanting to add the the population*

Some women are forced to have an abortion because of the political system and close family members.

After much thought a good many of these women had made this decision with a heavy heart. Most of these decisions are based on selfishness, self-love and are made for human convenience and personal reputation. The decision to abort are made without an understanding of re-incarnation and with very little faith in Gods' abundance. But there is a solution if the woman would fervently request divine intervention.

Every person must be taught the laws of karma. Every soul who attempts to take embodiment must be shown the importance of it. To work out his/hers karma every soul needs a body. This soul selects the family that will best allow him/her to fulfill that karma. If the soul is aborted, by the parents, it has to wait a long time for another opportunity with a different family. If by chance the soul is born to the same family that had aborted him/her before this soul brings along added layers of resentment or a sense of conflicts as a direct result of the abortion.

Abortion should never become a issue between the conservatives and liberals. It must be understood that all life begins at conception and should never be destroyed. Overpopulating the earth is the least of our problems because there are God-solutions for this. Ingratitude, greed, selfishness, prejudice, hatred, lust and pride can destroy us.

God in his infinite mercy forgives the souls that deeply regret their decision to abort and in his justice provides a way to make amends.

Do not abide in a sense of unworthiness or condemn yourself. If you have aborted a child. This will do nothing for you or for God. Instead look for ways to honor and serve life.

CHAPTER 11

On Working With Children and Youth

*H*ERE ARE SOME THINGS that you should know about heaven. Every right decision to do the 'good' and the 'right' is worth every sacrifice to enjoy the beauty of this realm. A place in heaven must be earned and cannot be stormed. Being falsely religious means nothing in heaven.

In the deepest sense it is extremely important to be who you are. Being yourself can only be accomplished if you can face your behavior and its accompanying habits and achieve the proper balance in your spiritual life. Without giving to others you cannot become with your higher self. Finding out who you are can begin when you give to others. This is part of the equation, not the whole equation but part of it.

If your life is centered on your lower self, you can only move progress so far. It is important to give children the opportunity to be of service to others. Giving children these opportunities is part of the early development of the heart.

It is very imperative to develop right judgment. This is a part of wisdom's flame. The children can be helped with this by having the opportunity to expand the potentials of strong habits of the heart and mind. Habits of the mind involve developing a love for qualities such as excellence, persistence and thoroughness. A result of good character is wise judgment. Good character must be fostered by school, community, parents and of course, church. To practice what they have heard about good character, children must be given the opportunity. Respect for children help them grow in alignment with Gods' principles as indulgence of children is never helpful. The way we treat our children or any other child in our care is part of the way we are tested and measured.

There is a mantle of adulthood that must be worn and developed. You must be a role model to every young person who touches your life. Not everybody is meant to have children but each and everyone of us is meant to honor the child and his/her God-given potential. Make an honest assessment of your life and where you are heading. With sincerity and joy you must come to deserve the 'good' and practice moral goodness in your everyday life.

Teenagers

There are no limits when you hold the sinless ideas by holding the Christ for another.

Most people do not understand clearly that there must be limits on our everyday living. People's souls need to be accountable. Children watch us very carefully and closely and they learn when there are clear consequences. There are many parents who shield their children at all cost from the lessons that would help shape their characters. Anyone who can discern the heart knows the difference between someone who judges our youth and endures tolerance and someone who is reporting the truth concerning observed behavior.

If we shield another person from his/her karma with human sympathy it is a great dis-service. True obedience helps to mold future disciples if it is based on love, power and wisdom. Many times parents protect themselves from looking within because they are unable to see the wrong their children do. Each and everyday, without fail, we should pray for the victory of our youth. Everyone should find some way to render service to protect the purity and innocence of our youth.

Holy Charity

Our youth need to have the opportunity to give to others, at a Goodwill, senior citizens organization or church food pantry. There are so many ways the youth can be of service. To see the level of charity each person should examine hi/her life. We are outside the circle of charity every time we condemn, criticize or gossip about about another person. If we are one who criticizes often you need to find the cause and core to find out why you need to do this. The way of the saints is to hold the sinless concept.

The youth of today need to experience the joy and meaning of giving. Giving will help the youth expand their hearts and their sense of being a significant member of the community.

Working with Teenagers

Our teenagers are very judgmental of adults around them. They are not deceived by words. These young adults look for mature adults who can't be manipulated. Teens look for adults with joy, balance and control. On a soul level teens recognize the 'true' parent or the righteous adult, no matter how they behave personally and no matter what they claim to want.

Every parent should ask themselves this question: *"Have I been a good model for my child?"*

If parents have been fanatical or hypocritical in their practices, this will have a great influence on their children. Children notice everything and more often than no internalize more than we realize as they notice everything.

Parents: Do not live in fear of your childrens every action. Parents make mistakes like everyone else and to be honest with yourself is very important.

If parents are religious and love their child they will naturally want that child to embrace their religion. Parents who wait under they are adults feel their children are fortunate to be raised in those beliefs. But the most important thing to remember is that parents have to understand parenting and have respect for their children. As parents they need to know the best way to impart religious beliefs to their child.

Each and every child born is unique. Some have a natural affinity for spirituality and want to follow in the footsteps of Jesus, while others are influenced by the world and find it hard to have a family that is strongly rooted in their religious beliefs.

Being a teenager is mighty hard for they are bombarded from every direction with unrealities. They will not forget receiving a strong foundation of balance and reality in their earlier years because it is recorded in their souls. Even after they get older and leave the church, for a while, they are more likely to return. Give your child the freedom to study other faiths. Ultimately, they are the ones who will need to select a church because no one else can do it for them.

The world calls and we are tested. Many will be deceived, but there will be a rare few so have God-vision at all times.

The greater concern is not with the teens but with the level of good parenting they have experienced. Children must see the fruits of religion in their parents everyday and see the fruits being put to practical use. In the greater context of faith there must be a bonding of family.

Give our teenagers the freedom to select their spiritual path. Throughout the early years of a child's life it is the parents obligation to lay the spiritual foundation. From how their parents live children learn more about religion than by what they say.

VERY, VERY IMPORTANT FACT:

Religion cannot be all Do's and Don'ts!! Religion must have joy, practicality, kindness, love, responsibilities and discipline. Children must have family time and fun time so they can have something to look back on. Family rituals are very important and equally important is feeling listened to.

As a family parents and children should pray, say grace, attend Sunday school and church together. An important part of family life is worship. Children experience the many ways that praying can help in a person's daily life from seeing that faith is the foundation of their parent' lives.

What should be emphasized in our schools?

Children must be made to believe in their God given potentials. They are exposed to the principle of moral standards. Our children must see the role of learning as a necessity for their growth and they need to feel that they have a desired goal in their studies.

Our school systems need the power of prayer. This important tie to God, that helped protect the schools for many years has been removed. The public school administrators feel that an acknowledgment of God would be harmful to our youth.

We desperately need to get the parents involved in the education of their children. The presence of ethics and deep moral values are very critical in this modern-electronic world. By personal opportunities to take part in 'doing good' our youth learn from role models.

Being a role model must be emphasized to parents and schools. Our system is flawed and must be changed. To change the system it will have to involve parents, teacher training and God.

We as a civilized world are judged on how we care for our growing children and not only are we responsible for our immediate family, but we are also a part of the family of God.

Adopting:

It is not possible or practical for everyone to adopt a child but the avenue of prayer is always available. Pray for the protection of the purity and innocence of our youth.

The list for adoption is long. But for the parent and child alike this can be one of the most heart wrenching moments of their lives.

Civilization is judged on how we care for our young.

Even though we cannot adopt there are other avenues such as giving to help children, but most of all prayer is available. These prayers can be offered on behalf of the protection of the purity and innocence of our youth.

There are adoption angels. Their purpose is to connect prospective parents, through parenthood, with the souls they are meant to minister to. This connection does not always happen because the prospective parents have free will and can reverse a situation that was meant to happen. If you have done the spiritual work, even if it doesn't work out, remember that you will not get a soul that is not intended for you.

There are numerous souls of light to be adopted. Also there are souls with challenging karma and momentums and a part of this equation will be your own karma. The violet flame provides you with the privilege of sponsoring a very special soul. Adoption may seem complicated but it can bring you the same soul as a natural birth would have.

As children, who have been adopted, grow they wish to seek out their birth parents. Some are able to find their birth parents while others can't because their birth parents have died. Whatever happens is usually a direct result of the karma. Do not fear this but understand it as a fulfilling of the law. Whether or not you adopt let your actions be guided by the hand of God that never fails.

On Behalf of Our Youth

Our youth must be saved and you cannot pray enough for the future of our youth. Untold numbers of our young people are confused, angry and lacking in hop or clear values. They should not be like this.

Innocence is beautiful before God. Purity is the way of God. Our civilization has exposed our youth to so many things that are impure and corrupted at early ages.

REMEMBER:

Civilization is measured by the care of its young and elderly. The care that is measured is their souls. It is possible to have a youth-oriented society in which no attention is paid to the soul and its growth.

Focusing solely on the health and victory of your family and relatives is an imperfect idea. We must be thoughtful, loving and honorable in our relationships with those closest to us but we cannot neglect our responsibility to life itself. We should seek spiritual and physical ways to help solve the planets problems even if we have a karma and dkarma with those closest to us.

How can we reverse the poverty and abandonment of children worldwide?

Jesus could not have made it clearer about his respect for the little children. People have allowed a hardness of heart and a spiritual blindness to penetrate their being when they have grown insensitive to the plight of children. People are making karma by the ways in which they neglect the children.

Human rights should begin with the right treatment of children. Nothing defies God-solution. If all the religions would unite and band together in prayer the solutions would start to come forward.

Our children deserve opportunities in their early years they deserve to know human love and care. They must be told of the way of light, divine purpose and of God.

Gangs

Many of our young people are misled by or forced into gangs. These gangs are like cancer which is growing in all the cities of the nation. Our children must be challenged and stopped before we are unable to control them.

For our decent, law-abiding living, our cities need to be brought back to a useful, good condition. We should support and encourage all efforts to bring safety to our streets and hope to the children.

CHAPTER 12

Social Conditions on Planet Earth

THE SOCIETY IN WHICH we live more often than not protects that which is harmful to people than what is best for common good. We are so afraid to be controlled or limited in any way that we have become suspicious of virtue and what it may ask of us. The just are not protected as much as the unjust are.

Many years ago our country was founded on spiritual principles. If these principles are eroded the foundation will fall.

Most people do not understand the influence the media has. For what they do not challenge this industry bears accountability. They have great skill in bringing you the astral level but there is little that brings you the higher way of life.

We live in a generation of technology. This technology is God-given but it uses have been left up to the free will of mankind and so often they have chosen the lower way.

Our children are growing up with a weakening of their auric covering. Just think of the music, movies and plays they watch and then ask yourself:

Would I invite Jesus, Moses, David, Solomon or any of the other great people of the Bible to hear or watch this?

Children need:
   a) **Time in Nature**
   b) **Time to be creative in arts and crafts**
   c) **Time to serve others**
   d) **Time to share in family fun and games**
   e) **Time to worship**
   f) **Time to study**
   g) **Time to exercise**
   h) **Time to read**

Being used as an educational tool or for positive entertainment at well selected times the media should only have a very small part of our childrens lives.

People are definitely drawn to the movies and plays that have explicit sex and violence. That is most want.

Whether through drama, comedy or musicals we need our plays to exalt and inspire.

In technology we need students who can make ensure that these inventions are used for good.

Without achieving this we will see an era like the sinking Atlantis.

Misunderstanding between the races

Desperation fills the world. There is so much hatred between the races and it is growing out of control. But our problems are not just between different races, as many may think. The solution to the racial situation is spiritual.

America is an experiment in bringing together the twelve tribes of Israel.

Is there anywhere else on earth that is as diverse as the United States? Where appropriate the wounds must be healed and the wrongs must be acknowledged. There is an important thing that we must remember and that is that we must rediscover ourselves as brothers and sisters.

If we have a 'we' mentality it will never work. If we are defeated from within it will be a sad day indeed. The uniqueness of the development of the mind can benefit our society and enhance the potential of what we become. This nation is failing to be an example.

Here are some forces you want to lose:

a) *to hate*
b) *to destroy*

c) *to fear*
d) *to accuse*

In all religions the Golden Rule is present in some form. This golden rule must be lifted up once again to unify us. We have a calling to turn around race relations.

In Matthew 7: 12 and Luke 6: 31 it tells us; "Do unto others what you want them to do to you."

We need to pray for healing due to racial hatred. People of all races and creeds could live in a wonderful world if we would find light in others. All of us have worn coats of many colors.

Words can be deceptively positive. Do not be deceived by the fallen angels who speak powerfully and compelling. Their plan is to destroy, divide and manipulate.

As we know Jesus never turned anyone away no matter the class, creed or race.

God has tried hard to impart the flame of opportunity but many have deafened their ears and hardened their hearts and many have suffered.

Once we have gone from this life and stand before the court of judgment, our souls stand naked before God. Our degree of love and our actions are measured. Neither skin color or culture is discussed.

Pray America will be a beacon of peace and freedom.

Now is the time for people to become accountable for their actions, words and for the cleansing of their hearts.

In America there is much ignorance concerning race and different cultures.

ALARMING:

On this planet there are more practicing Satanists than you can imagine.

There are a alarming number of people who have sold their soul in order to obtain what they perceive as a hold on power. Another alarming thing is the percentage of people who dabble in black magic, witchcraft and the ouija board. They are completely unaware of the dangers they are possibly yielding themselves to. There is a great number of young people who read books on these topics and become excited with curiosity and interest.

People who are experts in the areas of Satanism, black magic and witchcraft have a command of energy. These people have lost all their innocence and do not like, in fact they hate purity and compassion. They do not like pure joy or any other qualities of God. The people who deal in Satanism can only win if people remain simply and naive about their intent. We need to pray that God will give us the vision so these people will be exposed. These Satanists fear the eye of God upon them.

Satanists do not handle the violet flame well because it dissolves their power holds, disguises and manipulations. It is the very freedom of the soul that they do not understand and do not others to know. This battle over satanism will not be won without the constant and consistent use of prayer and the violet flame.

Are there enough souls to save the planet? The souls who are willing to save the planet must be willing to sacrifice to achieve this.

We are approaching the 'Y' in the road.

What can be said to wake people up?

God will give you an answer if you go to the inner altar of your heart and ask. You alone must do this without depending on others. Your example may help others to join the call. It will take every Christian to turn this planet around so that its divine destiny can be fulfilled. Intense and heartfelt prayers is required.

Victory is Possible!!!!!

CHAPTER 13

The State of the Planet

*L*OOK!!!!

Plan and be vigilant as we face challenges and great victories.

SEEK Christ attunement and listening grace.

Many of us are concerned about the future, are weary and doubtful of our path and of the need to be concerned about the planet. If you cannot read the signs of the times or have heard about them to often than focus on becoming the best you can be. Our path of decrees and prayer is the path for those who believe in the Lord Jesus Christ and who know that the presence of God is within them. These souls believe in the fire within their heart.

The energies are intensifying. People are often tested in ways that they have never experienced before as their energy intensifies. Than they want to blame God instead of looking at themselves.

Many of us can be granted the gift of the Holy Spirit. Our days may feel oppressive as we become close to God. BUT--hang in there, pray more, love more, serve more and stay concentrated on your spiritual foundations

Never allow your days to become overwhelming or allow yourself to get out of balance. The moment you lose your balance you are much less effective in your spiritual progress. Spirituality must be practical. What is practical for one person may be impractical to others. What you gain spiritually is reflected in your everyday living, your treatment of others and your attitude towards life and God.

Every time you call upon God, every prayer you say, that is beautiful, will have an impact for good and God.

You alone know how much you can give and still remain joyous and victorious. Begin each new year with an assessment of where you are and where you want to go spiritually. Be one with God. When you walk with God there is no room for fear, jealousy, criticism or any other perversions because your true identity is in God.

Have a spiritual plan for the year that involves every aspect of your life. Never let events determine your way and be the captain of your own ship.

If you feel like you have been constantly tested or confused it might mean you have passed the tests. Our spiritual progress wears many pretenses and our path is tailor-made for our soul.

There are many people who have become fearful and expect the worst while others feel they will be spared because they are the 'elect.' Well!!! My friends, that is not accurate.

There is a necessity for worldwide change.

What is needed is prayer and lots of it, the right actions, pure hearts, a return to God-government, Christ education and adherence to God's will.

The more people that live for God and his light sacrifice for its preservation, the fewer violent changes there will be. No one will be spared from these changes. If we obey and believe we will be given a means of survival. Our answers are always there if we truly see and sincerely listen. Hope should not be lost because so much more can happen for good.

Earth is dying!!! There is no need for it to die because this is not the time for it to die. The earth is in need of a heart transplant, so to speak, because it is like a body that is weakening. The purity of heart is what's needed here on earth.

The weather is shifting as the elements seek to hold a balance, waters and land are being polluted and plagues are spreading without the average person being aware of it. Nature calls out for your attention.

The earth is not at peace from the personal, environmental and planetary level. Just listen to the radio or television or pick up a newspaper and read of the things going on. Hope remains and things can change. The people who know better are not responding.

The rarest commodity on earth is pure harmony, positive thoughts and actions must prevail and the forces of evil must be challenged and exposed. Those who know the truth must honor and practice positive thoughts and actions. Your homes must become centers of light while our hearts must become beacons of light. The Holy Spirit must be more important to you than anything on earth has to offer. The wind of the Lord is blowing. Keep your attunement and do not bear to the left or to the right.

Everyone has a part to play and you have nothing to fear when God is your pilot. But on the other hand you have everything to fear if you deny, postpone or abandon the course God set for you.

Be ever vigilant of your own path and do not spend time deciding whether others are doing right or wrong.

Opportunities is still available by the mercy and grace of God, but this can only extend for so long.

Leadership:

When it comes to politics of our world leaders so much that is taking place is hidden from the public. There is questionable alliances, plots and deceptions, also empty words and promises. The world and its people are farther from God in this hour than we have ever been. This can be reversed by being guided by the ways of God once again.

Those who seek power above all else have no place in government. It is no place for those who claim to have integrity but yet slander and defame at every corner. Government is meant for those who are able to govern their four lower bodies--physical-emotional--mental and spiritual. It is intended for the ones who understand and live as servant leaders. It is suppose to be for those who have access to God-power because they do not covet the power of the world.

Our prayer for every nation, city, town and villages on this earth should be that God would govern.

Morality cannot be shunned nor immorality justified.

Luke 12: 48: "To whom much is given, much is required."

This is a spiritual law. The mantle of leadership is given by God. We are given leadership by God and we must respect and honor it. With this responsibility there is a pledge of duty.

Secondary to this position of leadership is human fulfillment and personal pleasure. God does not ask us to never be weak or never make a mistake but he does expect us to learn from our mistakes.

Pray for our leaders. They are under criticism, condemnation, gossip and challenges. Pray for our headers to be upheld, guided and protected. Pray for the ones who prefer evil to be exposed and dethroned with as little harm as possible to the citizens of our nations.

The day will come when people will long for a soul of light to lead them. Let us hope that when the day comes there will be leaders available and willing to lead.

A Warning:

For many the things of the earth have become more important than God.

Ask yourself this question:

In what ways has my daily life, family, job, hobbies, study, leisure become more important to me than God?

All else falls into its proper place when God is the keynote of our life. Things get out of balance and the soul becomes vulnerable when we put family, work, hobbies etc before God.

Action is the Key

Earth is at a junction where it will not succeed without God-vision.

God can grant a soul more opportunities when he sees the willingness of the soul to take wise actions.

Contemplate the things that you know to be true yet do not move you to action. Than examine yourself and find the reasons for not taking action on the teachings that you claimed to love and believe.

Seek the gifts of the Holy Spirit for many reasons.

In Mark 16: 18 Jesus told his disciples that if they were to drink any deadly thing it would not hurt them.

Saints can transmute anything that enters their body.

Mark 10: 27 tells us: "...with God all things are possible."

This is an important time to bless all that enters your mouth and that you touch. Pray before you eat or drink. You can pray to be protected twenty-four hours a day but remember it can only be sustained if your path and heart are pure.

Fear is never the appropriate response but being prepared physically and spiritually is always the lawful solution.

Why are illnesses on the increase?

Each one of us are vulnerable to a greater or lesser degree based on karma, diet, exercise and the wholeness of the four lower bodies. If you are depressed you are more likely to catch a cold, flu or virus. There are new strains of viruses more deadly and harder to combat. These are part of the plagues referred to in the Bible and come from a variety of sources. It is mankind's refusal to bend their knees to God that allows these plagues to exist.

Most of us only pray for healing when we are sick, but we should pray everyday for our health. The best approach is prevention. Pray the violent flame will burn through every cell and atom of our lower bodies clearing them of all harmful momentums and substances.

Delighting in riding the waves of our karma, the fallen angels, delight in creating things to oppose us. Our body cannot be counted on without proper care. Come to terms with proper diet and balance in the four lower bodies. Rebellion and wrong desire keeps people from facing their eating habits and their exercise patterns. Watching your diet does not mean you can't have a treat but have them in moderation.

Pray at each meal because of the germs and pollution in today's world. Give thanks to God for caring for our need to eat. Ask for purification for your food. Do this with water, also, because so many sources of water are polluted.

Protect yourself in public places when eating by praying for purification of your food. Charge your food with the violet flame asking for a change that is impure within it. You need to desire earnestly this control.

James 5: 16: "The effectual fervent prayer of righteous availeth much.'

CHAPTER 14

Creating Spiritual Communities

*O*UR HEART IS LIKE a seed that gradually grows into a rosebud, then opening into its multi-petaled splendor. Once a seed is planted, in proper soil, it needs to be watered, given proper light and nurtured in order to flourish.

When we desire to grow in the excellence of love we must begin at the seed stage. Having this desire is a highly worthy goal, but remember it is only the first step on the journey to becoming the full potential of the fire of love. The path of which we embark on is actually a difficult path. But it is precisely what we need.

Examine all that is anti-love that is within your being. These perversions can manifest in many guises.

Mild dislike is as much anti-love as are hardness of heart, hatred, lack of forgiveness, impatience, labeling people and never allowing them to grow or change and closing your heart to difficult people and environments. There are many things that can block love. These include resentment, lack of thankfulness, greed, fear, selfishness, lack of knowledge, conceit and judgment.

The next step once you have identified your weaknesses is to place them into the violet flame for change. You do not need to proclaim that you have achieved your goal because people will feel the energy of love radiating from your being. You, yourself will know it by the constancy of the fire in your heart. You can declare your love but "the proof is in the pudding." Your statement of love will be meaningless if you do not show your love. God knows the needs of his sheep and he has a listening ear.

People need steps and stages of love. This love cannot vibrate as false or be overdone. True compassion speaks its own language and needs no modification. "Be gone, forces of anti-love."

With all things spiritual the path of love begins with a willingness to look at yourself. Most likely you have been vulnerable to the forces of anti-love if you are always seeing spots on other people's hearts but not your own.

When the forces of anti-love is allowed to fester, you become restless and there is no peace.

Necessary Changes

Many act as if they have been hit by a tornado and parts of their lives have been sent hither and yonder. The spiritual test and divine plan for your life is to stay tethered to the will of God.

Remember!!!!

Stay anchored in God when great chaos seems to overwhelm you. Envision yourself holding the hand of Jesus, without fear and walk carefully but firmly.

If you make your spiritual progress a priority the rest will come forward. You will one day find yourself on a long detour from what you claim to be your original goal, union with God, if you mistake success in the world as your highest priority.

God wants you to be successful but do not worship the human over the divine.

If it is security you seek, place God first and the rest will follow. There are so many that place economic progress above their own path to Christ.

Never forget who you are and the divine purpose for which you were born, even though changes take place in your life. Stay tethered to the heart of the will of God and the things that are built around you will be secure, pure and one with holy purpose.

Communities

Heavenly retreats are communities of the Spirit and there is a rhythm and flow to how they operate. They vibrate with harmony and peace. There is no hiding of one's personal momentums or personality flaws.

Remember the light of God never fails, let it be your guide.

Among people there is no place for criticism or gossip. If there are any differences of opinion they need to be shared and worked out, but not with malice or judgment.

People want to feel loved and safe. In our lives and being we all want to feel the healing power of God.

'I am my brothers' keeper, I and my brother are one, I and my sister are one.' This closeness cannot emerge from a consciousness of judgment or criticism. A power is needed and must begin in our own hearts. Progress will not be made if we focus on other peoples flaws and previous mistakes. No matter how seemingly small, each person has something unique to offer.

Remember the story in Luke 21: 2-4 about the widows mite where her offering was counted for more than a larger donation given by someone else.

What is blocking your ability to be positive?

a) *Is it hurt?*

b) *Is it mistreatment?*

c) *Is it fear?*
d) *Is it a lack of skills needed to share and communicate with others?*

But all these things can be overcome, if you acknowledge and deal with them. All things are possible in God and only in God.

People must have the opportunity to learn, voice opinions and grow when patterns shift. This opportunity must be granted to all. It is a persons' freewill if they decide not to change. The key component of a pattern shift is opportunity.

Each one of us is accountable for the harmony with which we contribute to the process of change. It is very easy to find fault but oh, so much harder not to.

Community Unity

Community means "come-ye-into unity." Community is about coming into unity with one another. There is a flow and rhythm to how the heavenly retreats of the Spirit operate as they vibrate with harmony and peace. Each retreat is built on the purest principles of community and have their own unique focus, decor and rituals.

We will ultimately face ourselves and all that blocks our real selves. It is a joy to do so, as real freedom is our ultimate reward. On what level must this unity occur? It must manifest in all four quadrants:

a) *Etherically*

b) *Mentally*

c) *Emotionally*

d) *Physically.*

Community is first and foremost a spiritual idea. It is the design of the Holy Spirit for the sons and daughters of God. At every crossroad it must be infused with spiritual understanding and Christ illuminations. Do you know that community is not defined by people living in the same area, sharing day care or following the same teachings. Within the community these may exist but the community is really a unity of the higher selves of all its members.

Community is best sustained where there are excellent models, people who have united with their Holy Christ Selves, people who have the Holy Spirit.

Community is work. We must face ourselves and communicate. Sharing a genuine commitment to the same visions and goals is required. Where the Golden Rule is implemented the community will flourish. Communities are based on truth and respect. Each genuine community honors individuals God-flame. In the community of the Holy Spirit there is no place for gossip or criticism. The identity of the community has to be fueled by values and principles. A community where no one has achieved the balance of love, wisdom and power is difficult to sustain. Community is about building; Building is a step-by-step process.

Your community is meant to be an example of a true spiritual community where people abide by the Golden Rule. It should be holy ground where church and community are central.

Our pioneers laid the foundation for us and had a vision for the future. They often struggled and wondered if the battle was worth it. The resounding answer was YES, but it takes an honest assessment, personally, of where we are and where we want to go.

Building the community is not a job for the conceited, the loudmouths or the complainers. It is holy work for those who have truly borne in their hearts the vision of what this community can be.

CHAPTER 15

Becoming an Alchemist

OULD YOU BE INTERESTED if Jesus told you that your Father, in heaven, had provided a sacred science whereby every lawful gift could be yours. But this science would take great love, wisdom and discipline, would you be interested?

Without change people are vulnerable to misuse. Change can be used for evil, with great karmic accountability but on the other hand it can be used for gain through the creation of gold and perfected gems. You will not find honor with God unless performed in the context of helping others or using a very small portion personally.

Before the misuse of energy began, the earth could have been transformed to have abundance and enlightment.

Where does the process of change begin? It is often where we fail to look--within ourselves. Our attention is often drawn to other sources that might bring us happiness or give us a glimpse into the future. We are always slow to look within ourselves. Change requires the conquering of our limited self. Change involves creation. You must be in touch with your Higher Self in order to create beauty and responsibility. We need to understand and overcome our own behavior. As long as our limited self is in control you cannot achieve true spiritual freedom.

We face many detours and barriers that are place in our path. Some of these detours and barriers are:

a) *fear*
b) *anger*
c) *lack of self-worth*
d) *pride*
e) *non-resolution with family (typically parents)*
f) *envy*
g) *selfishness*
h) *ignorance*

Out of these come many other traits.
Thoughts like:

a) I will never learn a new job
b) No one will notice me
c) She looks ugly in that dress
d) I am not worthy of Gods' forgiveness or love.

Do you recognize any of these thoughts?

If you tape and hear back the comments you made for a month, what patterns would you notice? What is the ultimate source of these thoughts? Make an effort to challenge the thoughts and affirm the light of God within yourself and others. Admit honestly if there is any areas in your behavior that needs to be unraveled through counseling and apply the violet flame.

Remember!!!

Spiritual freedom does not arrive on your doorstep. It is earned. Beware of recipes for instant spiritual attainment.

God is the doer. 'Let go and let God.' With every problem we encounter we need to turn them over to God for a solution. Our higher self is available twenty-four hours a day. Most of us treat it like a pretty figurine that we take off the shelf and admire once in awhile. The highest gift you have been given is your Higher Self. This higher self is your real self and should be your best adviser or friend.

Think of your life in terms of multiple television channels and ask yourself:

a) *What channel am I on?*
b) *What type of programming do I select?*
c) *Is it a channel of human chatter?*
d) *Is it a channel of worry, doubt or fear?*

e) *Is it a channel of gossip and criticism?*
f) *Is it a channel of work and study?*
g) *Is it a channel of family drama and relationships?*
h) *Is it a human entertainment?*
i) *OR--is it a channel of your real self?*

Some people seek channels that literally connect them to the astral plane. Their connection to their real self becomes more and more like a frayed wire. Ultimately the wire severs.

To know your real self is a freewill choice that requires discipline and a desire to know God above all else. Ignoring your real identity you are deciding to be a wanderer with no clear anchor or vision for your life.

Changing requires the forcing out of all selfishness.

The behavior of our limited selves stares us in the face each day, yet we become comfortably adapted to these momentums that we either feel helpless to change them or fail to challenge them.

In God, All Things Are Possible!!!

All changes are possible but we must take the first step to end our bondage to the not-self. We need to pray to be shown obstacles that are holding us back from our spiritual progress. Self-mastery is the key to change and it is also the key to our Christhood.

May you know the joy of overcoming.

We must break the molds that limit us, that cause us to say that the impossible cannot be and the invisible cannot be.

Arising from theses characteristics are unhappiness and negative characteristics. Think about the experiences that have shaped you in this lifetime. Now which of these experiences have you allowed to keep you in a form of bondage?

a) Live in the now, the present
b) Believe change can take place
c) Believe in the possibility of heaven on earth
d   Seek the will of God.

It is not difficult to break the old mold when your personal mission is clear.

Rejoice as you face what has seemed impossible as you truly put on the cloak of your Christhood and leave the old man behind.

As you study your changes it will help you clarify your mission statement for this life and you need to be very clear about what you want to accomplish. Do not write a mission statement which reflects what you think you 'should do.' write a statement that is positively true for you. Facing the truth is definitely better than creating a falsehood to please others. Contemplate what is holding you back if you feel that your mission statement will be found spiritually wanting.

If you abide in the God Presence and Holy Christ self, then jealousy has no place in your life. If you are abiding in Christ, condemnation and criticism of others or the world has no place in your life. You restrict the power of God to provide for you in an abundant manner when you are jealous of others. You do not know God if you blame him for your struggles or if you see him as having favorites.

God is just!!

God is love!!

Nothing that happens is arbitrary. Our life may seem confusing and unwarranted if we not have an understanding of our physical action.

'Let go and let God.' Are you letting God be the center of your life, your every thought and deed? If we have true faith it means God is the pilot of our journey and we do not need to fear the course he takes us on.

Let God take charge so that you may know his abundance. Allow God to be the captain of your life.

Above all else to your spiritual progress is our understanding of freedom. We are not truly free until all we want and live for is the will of God. We are not free if we are desiring to be noticed, seeking riches and fame or seeking to outdo others. When we are free, we are truly one with the mind of Christ. A natural outburst of this freedom is the capacity to create. True creativity is of God, not of man. When you clearly see

Gods' plan and his desire for us to receive our rightful inheritance, the traps of the not-self seem obvious and ridiculous.

When we are in the midst of his chimera, it all appears so real. Numerous people limit God by projecting limitations on ourselves and our fellow man. Jealousy, for instance, is the false illusion that God cannot provide for you equally as well as he has for another soul.

In Genesis 1: 26 God suggested we take dominion over the earth. His intention was for us to do so with and in the mind of Christ. Instead, we have destroyed and damaged a large portion of our natural inheritance. Much of this damage has occurred through fear, greed, ignorance and a lack of good judgment of the difference between the voices of good and evil.

We can limit our karma. We limited ourselves far more than our karma has. Contemplate your need to change your life in order for the will of God to be the keynote for your every action. You must become one with the will of God. You'll experience a freedom that is the open door to the creative powers of God if you become one with the will of God. With God all things are possible.

To move ahead in change, it is critical to understand the concept of harmlessness. You have set up a boomerang effect when you hold harmful thoughts, wishes or speak against another in a condemning way. Sooner or later this will return to you.

We need to be free of condemnation and anxiety. If we let our emotions rule our lives instead of faith and we seek to control others, we are not free.

Keep an eye on the thoughts that try to overtake you or any thought that sneaks into your consciousness. See how it feels to go through an entire day without holding or expecting less than the highest. It is very freeing. Tests and challenges will still come but you still can be calm in the midst of the storm. When others see your calmness they will be drawn to your peacefulness and your expanding aura.

We have the ability to conquer doubt and fear but we first must master ourselves in order to have God-mastery. A lot of us resist the fact that we must master ourselves first, instead of running hither and winder to find contentment. We hold grudges for what others have done and have great justification for all our hatred and the choices we make. But the true spiritual way involves the conquering of facing ourselves.

People have a hard time in understanding the degree to which they limit their own progress. Every doubt, no matter how subtle places a barrier between us and God. To have an abundant life faith must be a twenty-four hour a day commitment. Mo matter what comes our way faith is an absolute trust in God. Faith is expansive and never limiting. Faith is the belief that the power of God can do anything.

Mark 9: 23: "...with God all things are possible."

You will be transformed in the process if you seek perfect love. perfect love sees the Christ in all.

Perfect love does not limit or share partnership with self-doubt or unworthiness.

As children of the Most High we have access to the mind of God but we must claim it. Much of Gods' inheritance to us goes unclaimed because we do not apply the principles that he taught us.

Fear is the opposite of faith. Fear is a perversion of God-mastery. Fear has insidious energy. It erodes the health and well-being of the person in whom it resides. Fear can paralyze. Fear can cause failure. Fear can block the capacity to learn new things and it can block courage. Fear is a deadly poison. The fallen angels have great mastery in creating fear.

Our response to fear can become a pattern or a habit. Fear must be fought at all cost. It has no place in our hearts.

1 John 4: 18 says; "Perfect love casteth out fear."

Every time we allow fear to win, it denies Christ within and the power of God to overcome.

Attempt to categorize your fears and examine them.

Let me ask you some questions:

a) Do you have fear or loss?
b) Do you have a fear of looking foolish?
c) Do you have a fear of being alone?
d) Have you sought counseling for any insubordinate or recurring fear?

CHAPTER 16

Divine Justice

*D*O YOU WONDER WHY you continue to have struggles and major tests? Look back into the past and see how many people have rebelled against God. The Old Testament tells us of many, many people who rebelled against God. Read through the Old Testament and you will see the numerous ones that have rebelled.

Many people felt annoyed with or lacked understanding of the sufferings that people had to go through. These very sufferings and the way they are handled are a just and necessary part of one's progression toward God.

Every dot and title of our karma will come up for balancing, but the violet flame can change a great portion of it. Some of our karma is limited by grace.

We are given free will to create and select as we wish but we are also given accountability. Most of us do not like our karma.

Mankind has strayed so far from a true understanding of divine justice. This understanding begins with a belief in karma and a divine system of accountability. The divine justice system is fair, merciful and accurate.

As much as we try to avoid it, manipulate it or sabotage it justice will have its day, be it through the instant return of karma or an event that will happen, even centuries later.

Once life was peaceful and justice reigned and there was no sense of 'haves' and 'have nots.' But mankind began to violate Gods' laws more and more, so restrictions were placed on them.

Many of us wonder why God allows such seemingly disparities to exist on earth. The age we now live in is a result of centuries violating the laws of God through the use of free will in small and large ways and a just system of accountability.

If you could spend thirty minutes with the ascended masters, what would you ask? What aspect of your life that might have seemed unjust is holding you back? Are there pockets in your life where you avoid responsibility or accountability? Do you truly have faith in Gods' plan for you and in the purity, honor and love that are the foundation of divine justice?

Our spiritual parents cannot grant us the same amount of light and abundance we were once given if we have been squandering the light or worse using it to oppose and defeat the purpose of God.

To ourselves and to God we are accountable. Our earth would be and entirely different place if everyone would believe they are accountable. Many people are blinded and deafened to the concept of divine justice. Some of these people err on the side of greed, lust and power, while others err on the side of human sympathy.

No longer is the scale of justice in balance. This system is in danger. Justice is predicated on certain inalienable principles. If these pillars are ignored or if we treat the system like a game, then true justice cannot be attained. Justice requires honesty under oath and honor over intrigue and the desire to win.

The true justice system treats all people equally and maintains fairness in the making of initial charges. The handling of the trial and the handing down of convictions. The rich and powerful can manipulate the system. The poor are its pawns. There are some in prison who should not be there and should be freed, while others should be there but have never been charged. When a case is televised it does a lot of harm because it hinders justice and creates false heroes. Televising a case does not encourage truth and accurate verdicts.

The American System has a foundation of good and worthy. Our judges should represent nobility within the legal profession and have an integrity all can acknowledge. But some of our judges, who wear the robe, are corrupted and are an abomination to the laws of God. There are a very few who are honest, fulfill their offices well and deserves mantles. The honest and just judges are often burdened in a way they do not understand as they help hold a balance against all that is corrupt and out of alignment in the system. The tentacles of its dysfunction make us all vulnerable. May the justice of God permeate our country and its courts.

Your word and honor is important. It is the lower self or not-self that allows a person to procrastinate and justifies not repaying that which wasn't ours to keep. If you cannot be trusted by your fellow men or women then God cannot trust you with his light.

If you owe someone it is better to pay something monthly, even if its five or ten dollars or even one dollar, than to let months go by without making a payment. The effort you put forth on repayment helps the change of the situation, acting in a way that is similar to the principle of the tithe.

The ultimate sin is to fail to repay the obligation and then get non-apologetic as if you didn't have an obligation. What is worse is to lie about the situation. Be honest with yourself. Every action you take you are accountable. Within your psyche bind all unreality, intrigue, self-justification and disobedience of the law.

Obligations or loans are themselves wrong but the terms of the obligations and the attitude of the recipients and the lender are critical. If you fail to repay a loan you block your abundance for years to come. You must live a life that has integrity and honesty as its hallmarks.

CHAPTER 17

Working on Astral Plane

ANY PEOPLE ON EARTH are caught in the astral plane due to strong momentums with alcohol, drugs, a lack of forgiveness, committing suicide and/or living lives that are focused on material things and not on God. There is so much more that the list could be endless.

The astral world is entwining and established firmly and it seeks to hold you in your momentums. It is devoid of spiritual joy, light and it grows denser as you descend to even lower levels of it. Being trapped on the astral level is like a prison sentence.

Many of us take for granted the great light in heaven, thus it causes a slowness to change and we become less clear about the great opportunities in store for us if we are able to advance.

Working on this earthly plane is not simple or is it a leisurely task. Pray for the opportunity to help free souls from this earthly plane. Preaching the word is a way for you to change our overall behavior. This mission will not be yours alone because you will be the company of angels. These angels are there to stand by you and will not hold your hand as you minister to individual souls to preach.

It is very difficult to minister to people on the astral plane because being in the astral dulls the memory body and the ability to remember the light and true purpose of being. We become passive as the years go by and our souls cease to seek and search. Everyone of us is tied to someone. It may be your duty to minister to the souls you are assigned to help. Some find this work difficult--

WHY? Because the earthly plane can cause people to forget their ties to you and to doubt the true purpose of life. At its most intense, this makes for spiritual warfare. To the forces challenging you you must be deeply attuned.

What is real becomes unreal and what is unreal becomes real.

When a soul leaves the earthly for the heavenly, it is like a patient having a cast on for many months and then is suddenly freed from it. The healing is not instant but gradual. This adjustment is gradual and it takes compassion and understanding from others. The service rendered in the retreats are indescribable in its love and patience.

On the earthly plane work is very challenging. We are like spiritual warriors when we attempt to help souls. There are a lot of people who still blaspheme God and do not want to hear anything about the light, purity, holiness and all the great wonders of God. On the other hand there are some good souls whose actions have them trapped where they should not be.

People destroy their lives by the ugliness of drugs and alcohol. For their need for drugs people will commit crimes, hurt others and destroy their lives. This will tie them to the astral plane. The entities that people had on earth stay bound to them and have to be fought off once in another plane. Here or in another plane we have to fiercely fight these forces.

Matthew 10: 8 tells us to "...cast out devils..."

Through the use of drugs and alcohol we can lose everything.

The astral plane feeds the sense of worthlessness and loss of courage or hope to which people have become vulnerable to.

It is by love and light, the violet flame and the action of blue-flame protection that will set our souls free.

CHAPTER 18

Spiritual Path

HE PLEASURES OF THE world are so deceptive and so entrapping, yet they have no permanence. When we suffer for God it is like putting money into your spiritual bank account.

It is in sacrificing for God that we are born to eternal life.

For the salvation of the world many have been inspired to sacrifice. These people understand the need for and power of such deeds for the treasury of Gods' work. For their obedience and devotion they will be rewarded a hundred-fold.

Examine your life and look for something you can sacrifice for God. One way to sacrifice is to take time to pray for someone who is ill or emotionally weak. Make a commitment and fulfill it. Each person is unique so one persons' sacrifice may be another persons' daily routine and not considered a sacrifice.

Don't compare yourself to theirs'. Be honest with yourself and seek a forward movement towards God and a union with your Holy Christ self.

For Gods' sake a person who is truly on this path may ultimately suffer much in terms of persecution, health demands or sheer total givingness.

Ask yourself this question: 'Is this path worthy of your fear?' This is a path of deep love deep joy and deep purity. Only if you fear these qualities should you hesitate to embark on this journey--the journey to the heart of Christ. If you wish to know the heart of Christ and have it for your own, you must begin the walk with your steps of sacrifice. Each of you steps will be matched with drops of mercy and compassion.

You will suffer seeing the violations of the sacredness on our planet, if we truly have the love of Christ. At every turn the innocence and the purity are being challenged. The sacredness of life is not revered. The honor of God in government and in our justice system is steadily wearing away.

How great is your desire to know God through the gifts of the Holy Spirit? These gifts are bought with a price and that price involves the sacrificing of the human self for Christ.

Think on this:

If Jesus appeared to you and made a substantial request of your time, energy and abundance, would you turn him down or would you obey him? Your faith and the depth of your commitment to spiritual advancement as well as your attunement with the word has a lot to do with your answer. Pray to be available to answer the call of God whenever and wherever it comes.

Mary sacrificed as a young woman in preparation of her parenting Jesus. Joseph lived a sacrificial life before God before he was selected to be the father of Jesus. Jesus himself sacrificed much to come into embodiment and to fulfill a demanding mission that ask much of him at every turn. Out of much love and sacrifice Christ was born.

There comes a part in our life when we must choose whom we will serve. *God or mammon.*

Luke 16: 13: "...ye cannot serve God and mammon."

Our turning point is when we truly want God, want the Holy Spirit above all else and so many have never achieved this step. This is what distinguishes the saints from the exalted and respectable aspirants. These vital years call for a least some among you to want your Christhood and the sacrifice it involves above all else. You will not regret this life choice. ***BUT!!!*** And this is very important--this life choice is not for the faint at heart.

When our goals are absolutely clear and our sails are set for the kingdom of God, all can be accomplished and the suffering of the world can be endured. The more we give to God, the more we are given.

You and you alone can make the final decision on how far yo the mountain you will ascend. It is between your soul and god. We need to pray for strength and clarity of the purpose he has for us. If you are honest and sincere your prayers will be answered.

There are several levels in the heavenly plane and there are retreats that specialize in specific fields such as healing, science, art and love.

Earth is not prepared to the many ideas that are waiting to be released and could transform the earth. *It is dangerously unprepared in many ways.*

Here on earth there is misuse of every chakra and there is so much corruption and most often it is high places. Man is not ready to make judgments on all that is being brought forward. Some of the discoveries men have made may be a worthy vehicle of great healing. Others may stand as an abomination where it ought not to be. With everything that comes to your attention--*PRAY ABOUT!!* You must pray if you want God's directions and solutions.

Each of us has a unique calling. We should see Christ in everyone. Our very presence should be a healing force. We should talk the talk and walk the walk and live the teachings of Christ. Become aware of the dignity of each soul and show love. Be God's vessel. Be a pencil in the Lord's hands. God provides abundance when it is necessary to the work of a saint. Be free from greed, hatred, covetousness and other earthly weaknesses. Be guided through your mission with purity and dedication to the will of God.

Pray without ceasing!!

1 Thessalonians 5: 17: "Pray without ceasing."

Our advancement should be a path and process. The greatest pity is that some people do not realize that this path is open to all who seek it.

Holy Ghost:

The most important gift of the Holy Spirit is to pray for discernment. Without this gift of discernment the seeker is vulnerable to be moved hither and yonder and to the possibility of misuse of other gifts or not to recognize the true teachings from the false.

Which Gift of the Holy Spirit should we pray for first?

With the gift of discernment you know the vibration of truth and non-truth, good and evil, purity and impurity, holiness and impostors of holiness. When you pick up a book you will know to what degree of truth it contains.

On the Heart

Many who seek lack discernment and are drawn to books and to individuals who are not of the light. Every day we should pray for this holy gift.

People who seem ornery may be closer to Christhood than the one who appears polite and kind on the outside. The heart is at the center of everything and God alone is the discerner of our hearts.

If there is no or very little fire in your heart --you need to get past what is blocking your heart. Very often people misunderstand human effectiveness, a strong intellect and the ability to follow the rules, for good discipleship. Without heart breeds a mechanical mentality instead of true discipleship.

Our hearts can be blocked for a number of reasons. Even if you do not feel your heart flame, do not condemn yourself or assume the worst. But recognize that there is work to be done. Many people close their hearts because of traumas or painful events they cannot handle. There are many people who are greedy letting their egos cause them to be self-centered, often forgetting the plight of others. The Bible tells us we are our brothers keeper and as such we must bear one another's burdens. For all who seek God, your presence should be a shelter. This cannot occur without attention to the heart.

On discouragement

There is no more subtle force than discouragement. You may find it surprising but few people view discouragement as spiritually or emotionally dangerous. This energy can be used by the forces of evil to doubt God and abandon their true purpose.

The path to union with the Holy Spirit is not a walk at the beach. For you to attain greater heights on your walk you need to be refined by fire, for this fire brings challenges to your door. These challenges make you realize you need to depend on God. When we are in the enjoyment of human and physical comfort, this dependency on God is not likely to occur. We all need prodding. If Jesus felt moments of abandonment how much greater may our need to feel alone and without purpose? For the soul who acknowledges God's love, presence and accepts with grace the challenge that is before him/her this period is always shortened. When discouragement is allowed to fester and prevail the soul loses momentum and prolongs the test and agony.

Discouragement is the direct opposite of the abundant consciousness. It blocks the magic power and gratitude. Being discouraged people become blinded to what they have to do and what they have received because they are focused on wanting one event, person or state of being that they no longer see what they have already been given.

Accountability:

It is an appearance of the human condition and the lower self to wish to forget that which the soul knows in their deepest parts--their 'hearts of hearts.' it is the way of the dweller along with the temptations of Satan, to pull from our anchors and roots and to attract us to the obvious or not so obvious enticements of the world.

The soul is open to attack as long as one speck of an Achilles heel remains. Only by facing ourselves and our impulses can you be freed. There are times when other people are sent your way with the circumstance in which you are vulnerable. We are tested this way to see if we can recognize the serpent, no matter its disguises and to challenge the temptation.

Matthew 10: 36 tells us: "And a mans foes shall be they of his own household."

Household can mean our own community members, ourselves or those with whom we live or are related. The forces of evil are cunning. They will place challenges where we least expect them. They will use whatever they can, whenever they can.

Where does accountability come into play? We are not pawns of predetermined destiny. We have opportunities and free will. We have been taught spiritually on the outside and our souls have been tortured on the inside. Both are gifts and obligations. With knowledge and wisdom come responsibility.

People wish to make merry and seek comfort. They become experts in self-justification. They negotiate with God when they should be seeking to take notice of his words with thankfulness. All of us are accountable for what we have been shown and what we have learned spiritually. We can never judge someone else's path or accomplishments. We must walk our own path and constantly seek communion with God's purpose in our lives.

There is mercy and forgiveness but it is much better to listen to what you know and obey than to have to learn everything the hard way by trial and error. The more dangerous the times, such as we are now experiencing, the more important it is to listen to what we know instead of being like children wanting to play video games and being entertained while destiny calls elsewhere.

Every dot and title of our accountability must be balanced. When lessons are denied we make choices that we will regret later and regret is one of the worst punishments we can play with ourselves. Regret implies that we are suffering over a lost opportunity, something we could have done but chose not to.

We tend to beg God for events to go the way we want. By the equation of effort toward spiritual advancement and by the expansion of the heart, many events are determined. More can be granted to those who are becomers than to those who remain the dabblers or the on again--off again people. On earth commitment and dependability matter.

Many people on earth are not understanding how to balance livelihood, family and a desire to advance spiritually. A lot of them postpone their own advancement by debating whether others are making right decisions. Some become irritated or hurt by the treatment of their fellow seekers on the path. Difficult moments are part of being on our genuine spiritual path. We should focus on how to be of more service, how to grow in compassion and mercy toward life and how to walk in imitation of Christ.

A marriage partner, a new home, college degree or financial security are lawful desires. Put Christ first and these things will fall into place. In order to fulfill the call of dharma each soul has different things to achieve. Deep within your heart you know whether God is first or second on your list of pursuits. When you allow God to be first in your life, everything you are meant to have will fall into place.

On the heavenly side everything is so beautiful and amazing. Open your eyes to where the earth is heading without intervention and see what a difference you can make.

Many of you are surprised when you encounter difficult events, yet on that specific day that you encountered struggles you were diligently given your orders or prayers.

This can happen for a number of reasons:

The first thing is you must have as much accuracy as possible in your calls. Every aspect must be protected as you work on a new project or are hoping for a new job. Our prayers and decrees should not be global and non-specific. The prayers we pray should be precise.

Secondly:

What looks like struggles may be an act of mercy because you know something worse could have happened.

Thirdly:

All our important events are opposed by the fallen ones. Light will always prevail, but it is necessary for the battle to be fought. The fallen ones never go on vacation and they are hopeful that they can defeat the light through the forces of discouragement, confusion, temptation, lack of self-worth, lack of forgiveness, anger and gossip. They love to trap people in their karma. Light will always be the victor. Our solution--outsmart them with faith, hope, purity, love, honor, obedience, forgiveness and all of God's qualities.

Work to overcome your areas of vulnerabilities.

There is something important that needs to be said:

That is that many, many people pretend service out of an obligation or a need to appear good before men. True service is a state of being, a sense that you were born to serve. It is a very part of nature and you need it for the nourishment of your soul and the beating of your heart. *True service is a joy.* We ask God for so much and we depend on God for his grace and mercy. The genuine service of our hearts is what God ask of us. When you serve god with your heart, others feel it and are drawn and connected to you by the purity of your motive.

To some of us the Spirit of service comes naturally while others must have the spirit of service developed or re-kindled. Service produces meaning, self-esteem, responsibility and honor in young people as they are forming their identities in this lifetime. Very often we need the people we serve more than they need us. For every opportunity that we are given to serve we should thank God.

Jesus lived a life of service. Study his life for an understanding of the flame of service. You will be thankful beyond words for every genuine selfless act of service you have performed, when you make the transition.

Self-absorption is the worst deterrent to service. There are many people who feel their pain is too deep or their problems too large to give any attention to the needs of others. Beware of these state of consciousness overcoming you. Doing just a slight act of love toward someone else might help your own healing or your capacity to endure. There are some people so absorbed in their jobs or money making to notice those around them. You must know that no life is complete without service and that there are no conditions to use as an excuse for not thinking of the well-being of others.

There are some people who appoint themselves to sit in the seat of the accuser as critic of some of God's best servants. In some way you condemn yourself when you condemn others. In the past week what services have you rendered? What motivated these services? Who are you serving?

Internalizing the Word

There are so few people who understand the internalization of the Word. To internalize the Word you must become it.

Can you imagine what it is like for God to see us fail lifetime after lifetime because we do not comprehend the important truths? He has watched certain momentums of gossip, criticism, unworthiness, fear and pride recurring time after time.

Why do we hold on to these momentums? How is it serving us? What does it allow us to accomplish? Who is in control when we are gossiping or critical? Even though our karma may be blinded we do not have to remain in that state.

Pride can be blatant but in many it is subtle but deadly. Pride keeps us feeling that we are not worthy of Gods' forgiveness. It is this pride that makes us feel that we must do everything ourselves without accepting the help of others.

Very often we think we have to be helpful, be in charge, lift the heaviest load or do the hardest part of a manual job.

Self-justification has its roots in pride. This must be watched as a dangerous momentum and at its worst level can be used to justify the morally disgusting actions.

Only the will of God is justified!!
Seek his will!!!

CHAPTER 19

Teachings on the Path

*I*F WE ARE BEARERS of hope, guidance and chastisement they will transform the world and spare people much pain. Seek peace in your heart because through forgiving others and ourselves peace comes through. The path to this peace is divine love.

Praying, giving and fasting regularly are spiritual practices. Sacrifice in the interest of a better future forms of selfishness and self-love are greed, dishonesty and placing material things before God.

Can people of God not overcome their attachment to faulty teaching to recognize an emissary of God and his own son Jesus Christ?

The pride of the haughty and the materialism of the rich can be blocks to obedience, purity and a willingness to look foolish before mankind on behalf of God.

Twin Flames

Ascended twin flames cannot interfere with the free will of their counterpart who are still in embodiment. The flames make calls and hold a balance but they cannot protect the one in embodiment from returning karma. Every ascended person holds a desire in their heart for the victory of the lightbearers. The twin flame longs for the return and victory of the divine compliment but not in a human sense.

The one in embodiment may feel a profound loneliness, a sense that something cannot be found on earth. A person can be happily married but still sense something intangible is missing.

Solution:

Become one with Christ and fulfill your dharma. For every act of good and love you render others, you serve your twin flame.

In embodiment everyone seems to search for a twin flame. The best favor you can offer your twin flame is the willingness to face and conquer your human self.

There are many who sacrifice their path thinking they are searching for their twin flame. If you place the path before all else the twin flame is far more likely to find you or appear to you.

There are some marvelous souls with whom you have missions or excellent karma but the one you are drawn to may not be your twin flame, but love and honor him/her as you would your twin flame.

You are never alone even though your twin flame is ascended. You are spiritually connected even though you are humanly separated. Loneliness will fade when you seek the spiritual connection.

When love is missing, being angry with or judging a person will not change things. Attempting to supply the missing love is the ultimate key to its emergence. The best way to learn of love is to experience true love from the heart of another. To be accused or punished for lacking love will never bring about the transformation that love itself can provide.

It is God-quality to be organized. Organization allows everything to flow with interruption or delay. A God-oriented organizer is open to suggestions for change and creativity. Organization provides a framework by which progress can more easily happen than it can in an atmosphere of constant chaos.

If you were to die today, what would others say about you? What example would you leave behind?

So much of our life is determined by day to day living and overcoming of the obstacles that are set in our path.

Most Important:

Treasure the hours you are given and assess the use of your hours.

Do not let your psychology keep you from the progress you are meant to achieve. Right decisions are celebrated in heaven are light. Faulty decisions are a baggage, a burden that can be transmitted.

Make your decisions count for light.

CHAPTER 20

Colors

FAITH WANTED ME TO add this chapter in about colors. She wanted us to understand these colors and their meaning.

After the flood God appeared to Noah and placed a rainbow in the sky. This rainbow was much more than a phenomenon.

In the seven colors, beginning with red and ending with purple, God was exhibiting a natural miracle that demonstrated the complete redemption of man. From Genesis to Revelation the Word of God is full of biblical color meaning. We use colors to express how we feel towards God. Colors can be therapeutic and beneficial to us and a blessing to Gods' people. When we enjoy worshiping the Lord he enjoys receiving our worship. Blessing, strengthening, and uplifting the body of Christ uplifts and unifies the Lord's work. Our Lord Jesus Christ loves colors. The colors we see here on earth are only a portion of what we will see in heaven. I pray the explanation of the colors will release in you a deep understanding of the impact color brings.

Genesis 9: 13: "I do set my bow in the cloud..."

Here are the explanation of the colors as Faith relayed them to me.

RED

Isaiah 1: 18: "...though your sins be as scarlet, they shall be as white as snow, though they be red like crimson, they shall be as wool."

Red symbolizes:
a) *blood atonement*
b) *sacrifice of Christ's blood*
c) *covenant of grace*
d) *cleansing justification*
e) *sin*
f) *atonement*
g) *the wrath of God*
h) *judgment*
i) *death*
j) *love*
k) *life*
l) *the earth*
m) *redemption*

n) *sacrifice*
o) *consuming fire*
p) *the person of Jesus*
q) *the cross*
r) *refers to flesh*
s) *blood of life*

Here are some verses pertaining to red.

Revelation 12: 3: "behold a red dragon."

Numbers 19: 2: "...that they bring thee a red heifer without spot..."

Proverbs 31: 21: "...all her household are clothed with scarlet."

Red cannot be formulated by mixing any other color together.

"OUDEM" is a Hebrew word meaning 'red clay.' It is the root word from the name Adam, Esau and Edom, all speak of flesh.

Burgundy:
a) *the red earth*
b) *selfish*
c) *covetous sin*
d) *copper and gold*
e) *washing by the word*
f) *right standing*

Rose--Pink:
a) *Messiah*
b) *glory*
c) *Rose of Sharon*
d) *the Father's heavenly care over the Lilies of the Field---His children*

JESUS LOVES ME !!!

This statement symbolizes right relationships, heart of flesh, intimacy and child-like faith.

Romans 3: 25: "Whom God hath set forth to be a propitiation through faith in His blood, to declare his righteousness for the remission of sins that are past, through the forbearance of God."

Matthew 18: 3-5:...Verily, I say unto you, Except ye be converted and become as little children, ye shall not enter into the kingdom of heaven. Whosoever therefore shall humble himself as this little child, the same is greatest in the kingdom of God. And whoso shall receive one such little child in my name, receiveth me."

1 Peter 5: 5-6: "Likewise ye younger submit yourselves unto the elder. Yea all of you be subject one to another and be clothed with humility: for God resisteth the proud and giveth grace to the humble. Humble yourselves therefore under the mighty hand of God, that he may exalt you in due time."

Revelation 19: 8: "And to her was granted that she should be arrayed in fine linen, clean and white; for the fine linen is the righteousness of saints."

Song of Solomon 1: 2: "Let him kiss me with the kisses of his mouth; for thy love is better than wine."

Ezekiel 11: 19: "And I will give them one heart and I will put a new spirit within you and I will take the stony heart out of their flesh and will give them an heart of flesh."

Fuchsia:
(a vivid purplish red color)
a) *joy*
b) *right relationships*
c) *compassion*
d) *heart of flesh*
e) *passion for Jesus*
f) *the bridegrooms heart*
g) *koinonea (heartbeat of life)*

Plum:
a) *richness*
b) *abundance*
c) *infilling of the Holy Spirit*

Gold or Yellow: *(is primary. Speaks of trial and purging)*
   And ha) symbolizes the Glory of God
   b) divine nature
   c) holiness
   d) eternal deity
   e) the Godhead
   f) Purification
   g) majesty
   h) righteousness
   i) divine light
   j) kingliness
   k) trial by fire
   l) mercy
   m) power
   n) His deity
   o) Glory

1 Peter 1: 7: "That the trial of your faith being much more precious than of gold that perisheth, though it be tried by fire might be found unto praise and honor and glory at the appearing of Jesus Christ."

Revelation 3: 18: "I counsel thee to buy of me gold tried in the fire that thou mayest be rich; and white raiment that thou mayest be clothed and that shame of thy nakedness do not appear and anoint thine ears with eyesalve, that thou mayest see."

Revelation 4: 4: "And round about the throne were four and twenty seats and upon the seats I saw four and twenty elders sitting, clothed in white raiment and they had on their heads crowns of gold."

Malachi 3: 3: "And he shall sit as a refiner and purifier of silver and he shall purify the sons of Levi and purge them as gold and silver, that they may offer unto the Lord an offering of righteousness."

Yellow
Gods' Glory
Ezekiel 1: 4: "And I looked and behold a whirlwind came out of the north, a great cloud and a fire enfolding itself and a brightness was about it and out of the midst thereof as the color of amber, out of the midst of the fire."

Brightness of Christ
Revelation 21: 23: "And the city had no need of the sun, neither of the moon, the shine in it, for the glory of God did lighten it and the Lamb is the light thereof."

God's fire
Hebrews 12: 29: "For our God is a consuming fire."

Judgment
Genesis 19: 24: "Then the Lord rained upon Sodom and upon Gomorrah brimstone and fire from the Lord out of heaven."

Color of Gold

Psalm 68: 13: "Though ye have lien among the pots, yet shall ye be as the wings of a dove covered with silver and her feathers with yellow gold."

Amber

a) *Glory of God*

b) *The Fathers heavenly care*

c) *fiery passion*

d) *flaming throne of God*

Green

Growth, vegetation or fertility.

Pastures:

Psalms 23: 2: "He maketh me to lie down in green pastures...."

Marriage bed:

Song of Solomon 1: 16: "...thou art fair, my beloved, yea, pleasant: also our bed is green."

Papyrus plant:

Job 8: 16: "He is green before the sun and his branch shooteth forth in his garden."

Trees:

Luke 23: 31: "For if they do these things in a green tree, what shall be done in the dry?"

Blue

Refers to the sky, heaven and the Holy Spirit.

Exodus 24: 10: "And they saw the God of Israel and there under his feet as it were a paved work of sapphire stone and as it were the body of heaven in his clearness."

John 4: 24: "God is a Spirit and they that worship him must worship him in spirit and truth."

Blue can also mean water, the water of the Spirit.

John 4: 13: "...whosoever drinketh of this water shall never thirst again. But whosoever drinketh of the water that I shall give him shall never thirst..."

Lord's Commandments

Numbers 15: 39: "...remember all the commandments of the Lord and do them..."

Blue can also be for chastening or describe drapes of holy covering.

Black

Black refers to *sin*.

Job 6: 15: "My brethren have dealt deceitfully as a brook ans as the stream of brooks they pass away."

Disease

Job 30: 30: "My sin is black upon me..."

Famine

Matthew 24: 7: "...there shall be famines...'

Night

Proverbs 7: (: "In the twilight, in the evening, in the black and dark night."

Occasionally black can indicate health such as healthy hair.

White

Refers to *manna*

Exodus 16: 31: And the house of Israel called the name thereof manna: and it was like coriander seed, white and the taste of it was like wafers made of honey."

Righteousness

Revelation 19: 8: "And to her was granted that she should be arrayed in fine linen, clean and white; for the fine linen is the righteousness of saints."

Forgiven sins

Colossians 1: 14: "In whom we have redemption through his blood, even the forgiveness of sins."

Garments of Angels

Revelation 15: 6: "...clothed in pure and white linen..."

Gravestones

Matthew 23: 27: "...ye are like unto whit sepulchres..."

Throne of Judgment

Revelation 20: 11: "And I saw a great white throne..."

White symbolizes purity and joy. Also white can mean beauty.

Song of Solomon 5: 14: "His hands are as gold rings set with the beryl; his belly is as bright ivory overlaid with sapphires."

White can also mean costly decorations and wealth.

1 King 10: 22: "...once in three years came the navy of Tharshish, bringing gold, and silver, ivory and apes and peacocks."

Purple

Purple refers to royalty and kingship. Purple dye was precious and rare. An incredible amount of mollusks shells had to be crushed and processed to obtain the dye.

Purple was used in the tabernacle.

Exodus 26: 1: "Moreover thou shalt make the tabernacle with ten curtains of fine twisted linen and blue and purple and scarlet..."

Purple was used in the tabernacle and for the garments of the wealthy.

Silver and Gray

In the Bible the meaning of silver is truth.

Psalms 12: 6: "The words of the Lord are pure words; as silver tried in a furnace of fire..."

Old Age

Job 15: 10: "With us are both the gray-headed and very aged men..."

Beauty of Age

Proverbs 20: 29: "...the beauty of old men is the grey head."

Weakness

Hosea 7: (: "...strangers have devoured his strength and he knoweth it not, yea, gray hairs are here..."

Ashes

Genesis 18: 27: "...which am but dust and ashes."

Gray can be associated with sorrow, destruction, purification, mourning and repentance.

CHAPTER 21

Portraits of Christ

IN THE BIBLE THERE are 100 names ascribed to Christ and these names can be divided into four divisions.

1) Our Lord's Eternity
2) Lord's earthly life and ministry
3) Lord's abiding ministry
4) Lord's self-portraits

Magnificent Presentations
a) Alpha and omega
b) The Mighty God
c) Radiance of God's Glory

Warm and human portrayals of Christ
a) Jesus
b) Brother
c) Nazarene

d) Carpenter
e) Jew
f) Teacher
g) Physician

Kinship
a) Friend
b) Savior
c) Lord
d) Our Hope
e) Pioneer of our Salvation
f) The King of Kings

Sublime Revealings
a) Light of the World
b) The Good Shepherd
c) Resurrection and the Life
d) The Way
e) Bright Morning Star

What is in a name? A name is a very important part of a person and is more than a label of identification.

In the Bible a name had a significant meaning. Often names could denote characteristics or something related to the history of the person or his time.

A new name was given to signify a change of character or a period of time in one's history. For example God changed Abrams name to Abraham.

Genesis 17: 5: "Neither shall thy name any more be called Abram but thy name shall be Abraham; for a father of many nations have I made thee."

Abraham signifies father of a multitude or exalted father.

Jacob's name 'supplanter' which aptly described his earthly life. His name was changed to Israel after his traumatic experience at Peniel. Israel signifies that as a spiritual prince he had power with God.

Genesis 32: 28: "...thy name shall be no more Jacob but Israel; for as a prince hast thou power with God and with men."

In Numbers 13: 16 we are told that Moses changed Oshea's name to Joshua which means salvation. It prophetically spoke of his work in delivering Israel from her enemies.

In the New Testament Simon's name was changed to Cephas or Peter, meaning rock.

John 1: 42: "...Thou art Simon the son of Jona, thou shalt be called Cephas, which is by interpretation, a stone."

The names of Jesus are so significant that there is no other name so great. One of his name 'Methusel' means, when he is gone, it shall be sent. This name prophesied the deluge. What a testimony to Gods grace and forbearance. God gave Jesus a name above every name.

Reading through the scriptures we will find over 100 names and titles for Jesus, gleaming like jewels of radiance and luster.

Why did Jesus have so many names? No one begin to describe or define Jesus. He is the 'Unnameable One!' defying definition and description is His glory and greatness.

The knowledge of Jesus is of infinite value and timeless.

Colossians 2: 3: "In whom are hid all the treasures of wisdom and knowledge."

The more we know of Jesus, the more there is to learn. Each name and title reveals some unique appearance of his person and his purpose.

It matters a great deal what we think about Christ, what concept we have of him and his ministry to and through us for us as Christians.

CHAPTER 22

Conclusion

GOD EXPECTED MAN TO create a heaven on earth because he created man in his own image. But men failed and things on earth changed and became arduous and dense.

The heavenly kingdom is like heavenly cities that doesn't have restrictions of time and space like we do on earth. God surpasses ordinary limits, as is all his creation and this includes the angelic realm and the souls evolving. As we reside in the heavenly kingdom we have tasks to perform, which is often on behalf of earth or any other systems where there may be life. Here in the heavenly kingdom we have lessons to learn and classes to attend. This heavenly kingdom includes music, meeting places, libraries, places to worship and much more. The heavenly kingdom is filled with activities which is for holy purpose, in honor of the light and our creator. Around the entire kingdom there is the power of God surrounded with a loving environment blessed by harmony. None of us are the entirety of everything that takes place in this heavenly kingdom.

Our bodies are heavenly yet they have form and dimension.

While on earth remember to face the lessons placed before you as each obstacle that you will overcome will be a cause for rejoicing when your time comes and you are transported to the heavenly realm. As you live your life on earth opportunities will present themselves for you to face. Each opportunity is needed for us to grab and transcend.

The love of God is beyond anything we think of as compassion or parental love. Words are not necessary here but yet when God speaks, it has authority, wisdom and joy.

My prayer is that you have grown and gained spiritual insights in the reading of this book.

Call on the name of the Lord Jesus Christ and bond with him and become one with him.

As you journey homeward may you know Gods deepest blessings and guidance.